THE
BOOK
of RUNES

THE
BOOK
OF RUNES

Read the secrets in the
language of the stones

FRANCIS MELVILLE

FAIR WINDS

contents

A QUARTO BOOK

Conceived, designed, and produced by
Quarto Publishing plc
The Old Brewery
6 Blundell Street
London N7 9BH

QUAR: LBR

Senior editor: Michelle Pickering
Senior art editor: Sally Bond
Designers: Heather Blagden, Sally Bond
Photographer: Martin Norris
Illustrators: Sally Cutler, Rob Sheffield
Indexer: Dorothy Frame

Art director: Moira Clinch
Publisher: Piers Spence

Manufactured by Universal Graphics Pte Ltd,
Singapore
Printed by Midas Printing Ltd, China

10 9 8 7 6 5 4 3 2 1

ISBN 1-931412-40-5

Fair Winds Press
33 Commercial Street
Gloucester, MA 01930
USA

Sheridan House
112–116A Western Road
Hove
East Sussex BN3 1DD
England

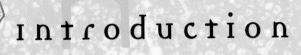

introduction

The runes make up an alphabet that was used by the germanic tribes of northern europe from pre-christian times until the thirteenth century. Rune is derived from rúna, an old germanic word meaning whisper, secret, or mystery.

Runes were used by the Goths of eastern Europe, the Anglo-Saxons of Germany, the Netherlands, and England, and the Danes and Vikings of Scandinavia. The Scandinavian tribes are referred to collectively as Norse and, since more of their writings have survived than of the other Germanic peoples, the runes tend to be most closely associated with this group. It is the Norse tradition that is explored in greatest detail in this book.

ABOVE Germanic tribes such as the Vikings traveled huge distances, spreading the use of the runes.

ORIGINS OF THE RUNES

The earliest surviving runic inscriptions date from around 200 B.C.E. In the Norse tradition, it was the great god Odin who discovered them. This is recorded in the epic poem known as the *Hávamál*, which is attributed to Odin himself and was first written down in Iceland around the ninth century. Scholars, however, prefer to believe that the runes were derived from existing alphabets with which the Germanic peoples came into contact. In 1874, Danish scholar L.F.A. Wimmer theorized that the runes were adapted from an early Latin alphabet around the second century B.C.E. However, there is little evidence of the runes being used near Roman lands at that time, although they were in use in more northerly areas

Etruscan												
Greek	A	B	Γ	Δ	E	F	Z		Θ	I	K	Λ	M
Latin	A	B	C	D	E	V	Z	H	Th	I	K	L	M

Etruscan												
Greek	N	O	Π		P	Σ	T	Y	X	Φ	
Latin	N	O	P	Sh	Q	R	S	T	U	X	Ph	Ch	F

ABOVE Many scholars believe that the runes were developed from Etruscan, Greek, or early Latin alphabets.

BELOW The eighth-century Franks Casket, found in the north of England, features depictions of Christian stories together with runic writing.

such as Scandinavia, suggesting that the two alphabets were not related. In 1899, Norwegian philologist Sophus Bugge proposed that the Goths adapted the ancient Greek alphabet to form the runes. Once again, the dates and locations of where the runes were in use throw doubt on this theory. A more popular proposal came in 1928, when Swedish scholar C.J.S. Marstrander suggested that the runes were related to an ancient Etruscan script from pre-Roman Italy. Several Roman authors refer to Germanic tribes living in the Alpine region of northern Italy around the fourth century B.C.E., allowing sufficient time for the runes to be created and spread northward by 200 B.C.E., when the earliest surviving runic inscriptions were written. This theory is supported by the nineteenth-century discovery of bronze helmets at Negau in Austria that bear Germanic inscriptions rendered in Etruscan script.

THE HALLRISTNINGAR SCRIPT

Those who prefer the idea of a more ancient heritage believe that the runes are based on the prehistoric script used in Neolithic and Bronze Age Nordic rock carvings, known as the Hallristningar script. Since such carvings have been found in Sweden, Germany, Austria, and Italy, it is possible that they have influenced all of the European alphabets already mentioned. The fact that so many of the earliest Germanic rune inscriptions are found in Denmark has convinced many scholars that the runes are essentially of Nordic origin.

NORDIC WISDOM

Although their precise origins are not known, what is certain is that the runes came to be at the heart of the Norse mystery tradition some 2,000 years ago. Although the last of the traditional runemasters lived in Iceland around 300 years ago, the runes can still provide direct access to ancient Nordic wisdom. Behind the doors to which the runes are the keys lie the realms of gods, giants, dwarfs, elves, and humans. They are places of heightened awareness where the game of life and death is played out to the fullest.

RUNE MAGIC

The ability to communicate complex ideas through the use of signs has always been viewed as magical by our ancestors. Writing in itself is a magical act, a way of manipulating the natural forces symbolized by the runes. The straight, angular lines of the runes are ideal for carving into bone, wood, stone, or clay. By carving runestones, or simply writing the runes on paper, you can use the magical and divinatory powers of the runes to access the ancient Germanic worldview, with its powerful connection with the elements of nature and the mysterious workings of fate and personal destiny. To believers in magic, the runes are keys that give access to the natural forces that they represent. The chapters that follow explore the mythology of the Nordic world, the meanings of the mysterious runes, and the ways in which they can be used.

ABOVE Writing runes on paper can help you access their magical and divinatory powers.

The runes are powerfully
connected to the forces of nature
and reflect the world in which the
Germanic peoples lived and their
mythological worldview.

1	2	3	4	5	6	7	8
Fehu	Uruz	Thurisaz	Ansuz	Raido	Kenaz	Gebo	Wunjo

9	10	11	12	13	14	15	16
Hagalaz	Naudhiz	Isa	Jera	Eihwaz	Pertho	Algiz	Sowilu

17	18	19	20	21	22	23	24
Teiwaz	Berkana	Ehwaz	Mannaz	Laguz	Ingwaz	Othila	Dagaz

The Elder Futhark

Rune-rows

There are several different Germanic runic alphabets, or rune-rows as they are known, all of which are closely related. There is much variation, however, both in the shapes of the rune symbols and the number of runes that they comprise.

The oldest of the Germanic rune-rows is generally known as the Elder Futhark, the word *futhark* being derived from the phonetic values of its first six letters, just as the word alphabet is derived from the first two letters (alpha and beta) of the Greek alphabet. As literacy increased and familiarity with the runes became more widespread, secular usage also grew, leading to variations on the original rune-row.

The Elder Futhark

The Elder Futhark, also known as the Common Germanic Futhark, is the rune-row most commonly used for divination and runestones. Its origins are lost in the mists of Germanic prehistory, but it remained in use until the end of the seventh century, when it was superseded by variants. It consists of 24 runic letters. Like Chinese and Japanese characters, the runes are ideographic—in other words, they represent specific things pictorially as well as associated words and ideas. The Germanic word *uruz*, for example, means aurochs and the Uruz rune is shaped like the horns of the aurochs, the now-extinct wild ox. Although there is disagreement among runemasters about what some of the other runes actually represent, it is nevertheless widely agreed that they are simple pictographs. The reason for this disagreement is partly due to the fact that runeworking died out in the seventeenth century, leaving only fragmentary literary sources to tell us what the runes mean. None of the literature tells us what the rune glyphs are specifically supposed to represent. Modern rune lore is therefore based not only on scholarship and tradition, but also on personal intuition and considered opinion.

The Uruz rune, which means aurochs (a wild ox), and is shaped like an aurochs' horns.

Pertho is shaped like a cauldron on its side.

Phonetics

The names of the runes almost invariably begin with the sound that the rune represents. The runic letters of the Elder Futhark correspond to most of the letters in the modern Roman alphabet used in English and other Western languages. Those that appear to be missing are mostly compensated for by other letters. The soft c, for example, is substituted with the s rune, while the hard c is replaced by the k rune. In Germanic tongues, the v and qu sounds are not used, while the letter y is replaced by j, the hard j being unused. The x sound is created by using a combination of k and s. On the other hand, there are single runes that account for sounds common in the old Germanic tongues, such as th and ng. Words spelled in runes were constructed phonetically in the same way that we use letters today, although, like Arabic and Hebrew, words were read from right to left. This is, of course, an important point to remember when deciphering runic inscriptions, but of less concern when constructing words spelled in runes for personal use.

Variations

All but three of the characters of the Elder Futhark are the same height and tend to the vertical. The exceptions are Kenaz (number 6), Jera (number 12), and Ingwaz (number 22). Later runemasters seemed to object to these irregularities and modified them to make them conform. The resulting variants can be seen in the four versions of the Elder Futhark pictured below, which are inscribed variously on jewelry and stone. Most of the differences in the order

BELOW These four alphabets show some of the variations that runemasters introduced to the Elder Futhark.

KYLVER VARIANT

VADSTENA VARIANT

BREZA VARIANT

CHARNAY VARIANT

and shape of the runes can be attributed to the preferences or even mistakes of the individual runemasters who inscribed them, rather than widely accepted variants.

RIGHT This fine example of runic writing was discovered at Maes Howe in the Orkney Islands, Scotland. It dates back to the twelfth century and was inscribed by Vikings who had settled in the area.

THE ANGLO-SAXON FUTHORK

ᚠᚢᚦᚩᚱᚳᚷᚹ
ᚾᚻᛁᛄᛇᛈᛉᛋ
ᛏᛒᛖᛗᛚᛝᛟᛞ
ᚪᚫᚣᛡᛠᚸᚷᛢᛣᛤᛥ

THE DANISH YOUNGER FUTHARK

ᚠᚢᚦᚬᚱᚴᚼᚾ
ᛁᛅᛋᛏᛒᛙᛦ

THE SWEDO-NORWEGIAN YOUNGER FUTHARK

ᚠᚢᚦᚭᚱᚴᚼᚾ
ᛁᛆᛌᛐᛔᚢᚱᛦ

THE ANGLO-SAXON FUTHORK

While the Elder Futhark was still in general use, a longer variant form established itself among the Frisians of the Netherlands and northern Germany and, more particularly, in Anglo-Saxon England. This new form became known as the Futhork, because the a rune, Ansuz, was replaced by the o rune, Os. Apart from this, the first 24 runes of the Futhork correspond to the Elder Futhark, with the o rune Othila being adapted to an oe sound. To these, another nine runes were added. The 25th is a rune called Ac, meaning oak; the 26th is an ae sound called Aesch, meaning ash tree; the 27th is a y sound, probably meaning bow, which suggests that the hard j sound was now being used for the 12th rune Jera. The other six runes, whose meanings are unclear, also indicate the development of new sounds in the Anglo-Saxon tongue.

ABOVE The Vikings were the most literate of all the Germanic peoples and created many of the examples of runic writing that have been found.

THE YOUNGER FUTHARK

While the Elder Futhark was being extended in Anglo-Saxon England, in Scandinavia the reverse was occurring. From the early seventh century on, certain runes began to be adapted or discarded, and by the ninth century, this process had resulted in a rune-row that had shrunk from 24 runes to 16. This shorter rune-row is known as the Younger Futhark, of which there are two distinct variants. These are the Danish Younger Futhark (often misnamed the Viking Futhark) and the Swedo-Norwegian Younger Futhark, which was the one most commonly used by the Vikings. The rune forms of the Danish Futhark are similar in style to the Elder Futhark, while the Swedo-Norwegian Futhark, also called short-twig runes, employs many simpler rune forms. The reduction of the Futhark to 16 runes resulted in the loss of many sounds. The reason some phonetically crucial runes were discarded while other, apparently less vital, ones were retained is a mystery, particularly since the Vikings were the most literate of all the old Germanic peoples. A few changes were made to improve the situation, but by that time the use of runes was in decline and the use of the Latin alphabet was growing. Poetic and magical runeworking persisted in Iceland until the seventeenth century, before slipping beneath the waves of history, only to resurface anew in the twentieth century.

THE
NORDIC
MYTHOS

THE MEANINGS OF THE RUNES ARE CONNECTED
WITH FERTILITY, WEATHER, SUNLIGHT,
DARKNESS, AND THE CYCLE OF THE SEASONS,
AND REFLECT THE RELATIONSHIP OF THE ANCIENT
GERMANIC TRIBES WITH THEIR ENVIRONMENT.
THIS RELATIONSHIP ALSO SHAPED THE TRIBES'
MYTHS AND LEGENDS, AND THE RUNES
SERVE AS WINDOWS ONTO THIS
MYTHIC WORLDVIEW.

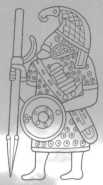

The Germanic peoples

The people who used the runes are referred to collectively as the Germanic peoples. They share the same Indo-European roots as the Celts, Greeks, and Romans, with whom they also had many beliefs in common.

Initially concentrated in southern Scandinavia, the Germanic tribes expanded southward in pre-Christian times. The main tribal groups included the Goths, who moved to the Black Sea area from the mouth of the River Vistula in what is now northern Poland; the Saxons, who inhabited the area now known as Germany and then expanded into Britain; and the Danes and Swedo-Norwegian Vikings or Norsemen of Scandinavia.

ORAL TRADITIONS

The Germanic tribes were all great bards—poets and storytellers—but they committed little to writing. Of the pre-Christian beliefs of the Goths, for example, we know practically nothing because nothing was recorded. It is partly for this reason that the runes retained their magical aura for so long. They were rarely used for mundane secular purposes. Indeed, as the level of literacy grew and the secular use of runes increased, the power of the runes waned and they were submerged beneath the Romano-Christian tide.

ABOVE A fourteenth-century painting in a Danish church showing dragon-prowed Viking ships during a battle at sea.

ICELAND

NORWAY   SWEDEN

DENMARK   River
Vistula

BRITAIN   POLAND

NETHERLANDS   GERMANY

BLACK SEA

GOTHS
SAXONS
DANES
VIKINGS

WRITTEN LORE

It was among the Norse peoples, particularly the seafaring Vikings of far-flung Iceland, that the old pagan traditions survived the longest. It was here, too, that the mother lode of Germanic mythology was compiled between the ninth and thirteenth centuries. This consists of two great collections, known as the *Eddas*. The *Elder Edda*, or *Poetic Edda*, is a collection of epic poems celebrating heroic legends and religious mythology composed in verse. The *Prose Edda* is the work of Snorri Sturluson, former Lawgiver of Iceland, and dates back to 1235. It is from the *Eddas* that we derive most of our knowledge of Norse religion and mysticism. Runic lore is therefore redolent with the windswept, salty savor of blood, bones, seas, and stones—the elements of Norse existence.

ABOVE The ancient Germanic peoples settled throughout most of Europe but their major strongholds were in the north. This map shows the areas occupied by the Goths, Saxons, Danes, and Vikings and indicates the places to which they traveled and took the runic alphabet.

creation

The Voluspa, one of the great epic poems of the Elder Edda, tells the story of creation, stating that in the beginning there was nothing but a yawning gulf called the Ginnungagap.

To the north of the gulf lay Niflheim, the land of ice, mist, and darkness; to the south lay Muspelsheim, the land of raging fire. Gradually, these primary elements formed glaciers that began to fill the gulf. Warm winds from the south began to melt the glacial ice, and the quickening waters of this first spring gave birth to Ymir, the first frost giant.

ABOVE Audhumla the cow created life-giving waters by licking the glacial ice in the gulf of Ginnungagap.

BIRTH OF THE GODS

Ymir's first companion, born also of this primary fluid, was Audhumla the cow, the ancestral mother of all living creatures, who suckled Ymir with her milk. Licking the ice with her tongue, Audhumla augmented the flow of life-giving water, which produced another new being called Buri. Buri and Ymir both bore offspring. Buri's son Bor married Bestla, a descendent of Ymir. Bestla gave birth to three sons—Odin, Vili, and Ve, the first gods. The gods and giants became adversaries in incessant conflict.

THE SLAYING OF YMIR

The sons of Bor attacked and killed Ymir. His blood filled the rest of Ginnungagap and formed the oceans. From his flesh the gods made dry land, from his bones the mountains, from his teeth cliffs, from his hair trees, and from his brain clouds. His skull became the vault of heaven, which caught

LEFT Odin, one of the first three Norse gods, became the most important deity in the Nordic mythos.

LEFT According
to the Norse
creation myth,
sparks from the
raging fires of
Muspelsheim
formed the
celestial bodies
of the universe.

the sparks from the fires of Muspelsheim
to form the Sun, the Moon, the stars, and
the planets. The gods set these in motion,
thereby initiating all the cycles of time, such
as the four seasons and night and day, which
in turn gave birth to vegetation. From the
great bushy eyebrows of Ymir, the gods built
the foundations of the land of Midgard
(middle land), which lay between the icy
wastes of Niflheim and the eternally raging
fires of Muspelsheim. They used an ash and
an elm tree to make the first human beings,
Askr and Embla, who resided in Midgard.
Other creatures, such as elves and dwarfs,
were also created and given realms in which
to live. When the gods had finished their
work, the Nordic universe comprised nine
worlds—nine was a symbol of totality.

RIGHT Ymir, the first frost
giant, was slain by Odin
and his brothers. They used
the different parts of his
body to create the universe.

yggdrasil

In the center of midgard stood an ash tree of unimaginable size and strangeness. It was called yggdrasil, the world tree, because it formed the axis of the universe.

Yggdrasil's roots penetrated to the depths of the earth, while its branches filled the sky and overhung the nine worlds of creation. The branches were host to many animals, including a golden cockerel that acted as a lookout for the gods to warn them of attack from the giants; a great eagle with a hawk perched upon its brow; a goat called Heidrun, whose milk nourished Odin's warriors; and four stags that ate the tree's leaves and bark. Despite their predations, Yggdrasil was always in full, fresh leaf.

MIGHTY ROOTS

Yggdrasil drew its unfailing vigor from its mighty roots. One penetrated through Jotunheim, the realm of the frost giants, to the Fount of Wisdom tended by the divine sage Mimir. Another reached to the ends of Niflheim, close by the Fountain of Hvergelmir, whose waters fed the rivers of the world. This root was constantly gnawed by the dragon Nidhoggr (dreaded biter). Another root ended at the Well of Urd in Asgard, where the gods met to pass judgment and dispense justice.

COSMIC CONNECTIONS

These three roots therefore connected the tree to the three worlds of time: past, present, and future. The Fount of Wisdom contained all the secrets of the past; the ceaseless current of Hvergelmir represented the present; and the Well of Urd was constantly replenished by the Nornir, the three goddesses of fate who knew the future. Emphasizing the eternal tension between the nine realms encompassed by Yggdrasil was Ratatosk, a malicious trickster squirrel who ceaselessly ran up and down the tree passing false and abusive messages between the eagle at the top and the dragon Nidhoggr at the bottom.

OPPOSITE The world tree, Yggdrasil, was the axis for the nine worlds of creation in Norse mythology.

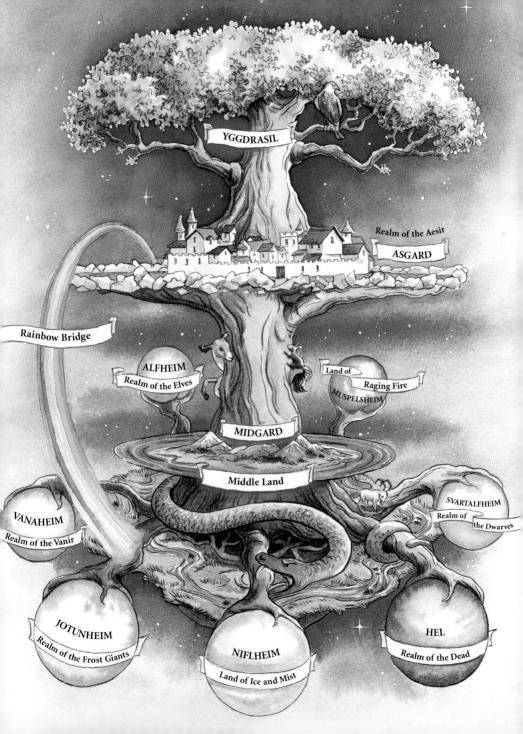

YGGDRASIL

Realm of the Aesir
ASGARD

Rainbow Bridge

ALFHEIM
Realm of the Elves

Land of
Raging Fire
MUSPELSHEIM

MIDGARD

Middle Land

SVARTALFHEIM
Realm of
the Dwarves

VANAHEIM

Realm of the Vanir

JOTUNHEIM
Realm of the Frost Giants

NIFLHEIM
Land of Ice and Mist

HEL
Realm of the Dead

the gods

The Nordic gods fall into two groups, known as the Aesir and the Vanir. The Aesir are the sky gods, whose principal functions are magic, wisdom, war, and law. The Vanir are peaceful nature deities.

ABOVE Thor, Odin, Frey, Tyr, and Loki. Frey was one of the Vanir race of gods; the others were members of the Aesir.

The Aesir include the best-known gods Odin and Thor, whose origins and ancestry are recorded. The Vanir are more mysterious than the Aesir, with no surviving mythology to account for their origins. Their chief figures include Frey, Freya, and Frigg.

LEFT The Norse gods were not immortal. They increased their longevity by eating the magic apples of the goddess Idun.

THE AESIR

Having established the land of Midgard from the body of Ymir, the Aesir employed one of the giants as architect to build their own estate, which they called Asgard—the land of the As, or Aesir. Asgard was could only be reached by crossing a great rainbow bridge called Bifrost and it became a magnificent fortified domain with sumptuous palaces of incredible size. The most glorious of these heavenly abodes was Valhalla, the great hall of Odin, where brave warriors who had fallen in battle spent their days preparing for war with the giants and their nights feasting in the banquet hall. Despite their magnificence, however, the gods were not all-powerful, and they were often outwitted or outfought by giants, sorcerers, and even dwarfs. Indeed, if they did not eat the magic apples of the goddess Idun to extend their lives, the gods would have perished like other mortals.

THE VANIR

The only members of the Vanir of whom we know are those who crossed the rainbow bridge to live with the Aesir in Asgard. This came about as the result of a great war between the two races of gods. Losses were severe on both sides, but neither could gain the upper hand. In the end, they agreed on a peace and exchanged hostages to ensure that it was kept, a traditional custom among the Germanic peoples.

RIGHT Asgard, the realm of the Aesir, was a place of sumptuous palaces and could only be reached by crossing a rainbow bridge.

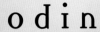

odin

The most important of all the Nordic gods is the mighty odin, god of wisdom, communication, and magic. He is chief of the gods in the Germanic pantheon, just as Jupiter/Zeus is chief of the Olympian gods in Roman/Greek myth.

Known as Woden or Wotan (the furious) to the Saxons, Odin appears to have been worshipped originally as a war god, in accordance with the legend recounting the slaying of the giant Ymir. He led the Wild Hunt, a frenzied band of ghostly warriors who could be heard galloping through the skies on stormy nights. As the patron of warriors, he received the bravest of them into his great stronghold, Valhalla.

God of wisdom

Odin achieved his virtues and status through sacrifice, cunning, and conquest. He was not born all-knowing, but his burning curiosity about the world led him to the Fount of Wisdom. The guardian of the fountain was a water spirit called Mimir (he who thinks), who was also said to be Odin's uncle. Odin wished to drink from this fountain to increase his knowledge, but in the old tradition of "an eye for an eye," Mimir demanded one of Odin's eyes in exchange. Odin accepted and threw one of his eyes into the fountain, earning himself the epithet "the one-eyed." The loss of his eye was compensated for by his two ravens, called Huginn (thought) and Munnin (memory), who perched on his shoulders and informed him of what they had seen and heard. The raven was therefore one of Odin's totem animals, along with the stag and the wolf, a pair of which attended his throne at Valhalla. Following his exchange of outward sight for inner vision, Odin left Asgard to travel the worlds in his continuing quest for knowledge. Usually in disguise—often wearing a wide-brimmed hat and a traveler's cloak—he asked questions of everyone he met and also dispensed wisdom, thereby earning his title of god of wisdom.

ABOVE Odin at the Fount of Wisdom with the water spirit Mimir. The two ravens above Odin's head gave him information as compensation for the loss of his eye, which he exchanged with Mimir for a drink from the fountain.

the nordic mythos 27

LEFT Odin riding his eight-legged stallion Sleipnir, the swiftest and bravest of mounts. In his right hand Odin carries Gungnir, a magical spear forged for him by dwarfs.

GOD OF COMMUNICATION

In one of his exploits, Odin used his customary trickery to discover the secret source of hydromel (honey water), a magical brew that bestowed powers of prophecy and poetry on those who drank it. Odin was revered for his wonderful eloquence and shared the hydromel with those poets he most appreciated.

GOD OF MAGIC

The epic poem *Hávamál*, written around the ninth century, records how Odin discovered the runes and their magical powers, thereby earning his title of god of magic. The image of Odin hanging upside down from Yggdrasil in willing self-sacrifice is strongly reminiscent of the Hanged Man tarot card, the essential meaning of which is illumination through self-sacrifice. Odin's magical powers included the ability to shape-shift into anything he wished, most often a stag or raven. He was armed with a magical spear called Gungnir, forged by dwarfs, that

could not be deflected from its target once thrown. His trusty companion was the eight-legged horse Sleipnir, the fastest and bravest of mounts, to whom no obstacle was insurmountable. Odin corresponds closely with Hermes/Mercury/Thoth, the divine genius of magic in the Mediterranean esoteric tradition. The fourth day of the week was named after him (Wednesday/Woden's day), while in Latin lands it was dedicated to Mercury (*Mercurii dies* in Latin; *Mercredi* in French).

LEFT The Hanged Man tarot card echoes Odin's act of self-sacrifice to obtain the runes.

ODIN'S DISCOVERY OF THE RUNES

Wounded I hung on a windswept gallows tree
For nine long nights,
Pierced by a spear, pledged to Odin,
Sacrificed, myself to myself.
The wisest know not from whence spring
The roots of that ancient wood.
No bread was I given,
No mead was I given.
I perceived the depths: With a loud cry
I seized the runes, then from that tree I fell.
Nine ways of power
I learned from the famous Bólthorn, Bestla's father:
He poured me a draft of precious mead,
Mixed with magic Odhroerir:
I waxed and throve well;
Word from word gave words to me,
Deed from deed gave deeds to me,
Runes you will find, and readable staves,
Very strong staves, very stout staves,
Staves that Bólthorn stained,
Made by mighty powers,
Graven by the prophetic god;
For the gods by Odhinn, for the elves by Dain,
By Dvalin, too, for the dwarfs,
By Asvid for the hateful giants,
And some I carved myself:
Thund, before man was made, scratched them,
Who rose first, fell thereafter.
Know how to cut them, know how to read them,
Know how to stain them, know how to prove them,
Know how to evoke them, know how to score them,
Know how to send them, know how to spend them.

HÁVAMÁL: VERSES 138–144

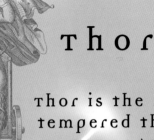

Thor

Thor is the mighty, hot-tempered thunder god, known as Donar to the Germans (donner means thunder in German). Huge and red-bearded, Thor is the epitome of the fearless viking warrior.

Thor was invariably armed with his massive, thunder-striking hammer, called Mjollnir (destroyer). Once thrown at an enemy, this weapon never missed and always returned like a boomerang to its master's hand. It could easily change size and be hidden in his pocket. It was also a sacred object that could be used to consecrate places and marriages. Thor's other magical objects included a magic belt that doubled his strength and iron gloves for holding the hammer shaft.

THE SERPENT OF MIDGARD
Thor was a skilled seaman, whose greatest exploit was the hunting of the serpent of Midgard. This was a vast sea monster that encircled the land of Midgard, its threshing coils whipping up great ocean tempests that could swallow the mightiest of ships. Thor managed to hook this leviathan and would have landed it but for the cowardice of his giant companion Hymir, who cut the line in terror.

STRENGTH AND COURAGE
Thor in many ways resembles the Greek hero Hercules. He performed massive feats of strength and endurance. On one occasion, he inadvertently initiated the tides of the oceans by attempting to drain a drinking horn that was attached to the ocean bed. For all his machismo, however, Thor's most crucial act was to fool Thrymr, the king of the frost giants, into believing that he (Thor) was a woman in order to retrieve his hammer. Thor had none of Odin's cunning and was often outwitted, but his loyalty and unflinching courage saved the gods from disaster on several occasions. Thor gave his name to the fifth day of the week (Thursday/Thor's day; *Donnerstag* in German), while in Latin lands it was dedicated to his counterpart Jupiter/Jove (*Jovis dies* in Latin; *Jeudi* in French).

JUPITER

Loki and Baldur

The most significant god in Asgard, after odin and thor, is the ambivalent trickster god Loki. Baldur is the god of harmony and happiness and was murdered as a result of Loki's trickery.

ABOVE The goddess Idun with her magic apples and husband Braga.

Although Loki sometimes helped Odin and Thor on their adventures, he was also a troublemaker with a malicious streak. This ambivalence came from his association with the vital, but dangerous, element of fire. Often described as a fire demon, Loki could transform himself into the fire giant Sutr.

THE CRIMES OF LOKI

Loki's worst deeds included the betrayal of the goddess Idun, whom he delivered into the hands of a giant, together with the magic apples that kept the gods youthful. His most appalling crime, however, was the murder of Baldur. In the end, Loki joined sides with the giants in the final battle known as the Twilight of the Gods.

THE DEATH OF BALDUR

The son of Odin and Frigg, Baldur was the most beloved of all the gods in Asgard. His mother tried to ensure his safety by making every living thing swear that it would never harm him. Disguised as a crone, Loki tricked Frigg into revealing that one plant had not sworn the oath. This was the mistletoe, which she had deemed too young. So, while the other gods were having fun hurling missiles at the invulnerable Baldur, Loki tricked the blind god Höd into throwing a dart made from mistletoe. The beautiful young god fell down dead. The devastated gods did all they could to persuade Hel, queen of the underworld, to release him. She agreed to do so if all living creatures expressed their grief at Baldur's death. Only one giantess living alone in a cave refused. The giantess was, of course, the jealous Loki in disguise.

OPPOSITE The fire demon Loki plotted the murder of Baldur, the beautiful god of harmony and happiness.

MISTLETOE

The Vanir gods were peaceful and benevolent nature deities. Frey, the most popular of the Vanir, had a magical self-steering ship that he could fold up and put in his pocket.

njörd and frey

NJÖRD

njörd is a fertility god associated with the earth and fruitfulness. His son, frey, is the god of peace and prosperity. Both were members of the vanir race of gods that resided in Asgard.

The Vanir were nature deities who ensured fertility, providing the rain and sunlight that allow all plants, animals, and humans to flourish. One of the Vanir goddesses, Gullveig, was seized and tortured by the greedy Aesir, who wished to extract from her the secrets of alchemy in order to make gold. The outraged Vanir demanded compensation, but the Aesir, who were mainly warrior gods, chose instead to fight, leading to a long, cruel war that ended

NERTHUS

in a stalemate and the exchanging of hostages. Njörd and Frey were two of the Vanir hostages who went to Asgard.

NJÖRD

In Scandinavian mythology, Njörd is male. In the historical monograph *Germania*, however, the Roman historian Tacitus relates that Nerthus, the corresponding deity of the more southerly Germanic tribes, represents Mother Earth. It may be that Njörd and Nerthus represent the opposing polarities in nature.

FREY

Frey, the masculine lord of nature, was the only one of the Vanir whose popularity rivaled that of Odin and Thor. He was worshipped as a phallic fertility god, particularly in Sweden, where his greatest temple was at Uppsala. There, sacrifices were made to him and great festivals held to celebrate spring, summer, and the harvest. Frey's magical companion was a wondrous golden boar fashioned, like Thor's hammer Mjollnir, by the dwarfs Brökk and Sindri. It pulled Frey's chariot through the air, illuminating the night sky. The dwarfs also made a magic, self-steering ship for him called Skidbladnir, which Frey could fold up and put in his pocket.

FREY

frigg, freya, and hel

frigg is the wife of odin and shares her husband's gifts of wisdom and divination. freya is the queen of the valkyries, who decide the fate of warriors, while hel is the goddess of the underworld.

Being a group of warrior tribes, the Germanic peoples laid greatest emphasis on the exploits of the male gods in their epic tales. Women, however, were greatly revered for their talents at healing, magic, and soothsaying. In *Germania*, Tacitus states that "they believe there is something divine about this sex." The gods themselves owed their longevity to the goddess Idun's magic apples.

frigg

Frigg was one of the Aesir. Her Germanic name Frija has led to her being confused with Freya, but they are two distinct deities. Frija means beloved or spouse, and Tacitus identified her with Venus. The sixth day of the week is named after her (Friday/Frigg's day), just as it is named after Venus in Latin lands (*Veneris dies* in Latin; *Vendredi* in French). Odin once said about his wife: "Only Frigg knows the future, but she discloses it to no one." Frigg was prayed to for blessings in marriage, although marital fidelity was not one of her virtues.

frigg

ABOVE Freya driving her chariot pulled by cats. She was queen of the Valkyries, female warrior spirits who selected those who would die in battle.

FREYA

Freya, whose name means lady, appears to have become a second wife to Odin, whom she even accompanied onto the battlefield. She was the queen of the Valkyries, female spirits who appeared only to those whom they selected to die in battle. Freya received half the slain into her palace Folkvang, while the rest joined Odin at Valhalla. Freya's beauty was legendary and caused her to be pursued by lusty giants.

HEL

Hel presided over the underworld, which should not be confused with the Christian concept of hell; it was simply the place where all dead spirits dwelled, regardless of their virtues. The only exceptions were heroic dead warriors, who served Odin and Freya in Asgard.

LEFT Venus, the ruling planet of love, is associated with the beautiful goddess Frigg.

The Nornir

ABOVE The Nornir pouring the waters of fate at the base of the world tree Yggdrasil.

These three sister goddesses are the spinners and weavers of the fates of humans and gods. They represent the triple lunar goddess, ruling over the three aspects of time: past, present, and future.

The Nornir lived near one of the roots of Yggdrasil, at the Well of Urd in Asgard. The well was named after Urd, the eldest sister; the other sisters' names were Verdandi and Skuld. Every day the three goddesses fertilized the tree of life, helping to sustain the very fabric of the universe.

FAIRY FOLKLORE

The three sisters were believed to visit newborn children and give them their special gifts. The story of Sleeping Beauty includes them in this role. The wicked fairy who predicts that the princess will prick her finger on a spindle shows their dark aspect and introduces the spinning wheel as a symbol of fate. The best aspect of the Nornir survives in the figure of Cinderella's fairy godmother, who allows the young girl to find her true destiny as a princess in reward for her innate

BELOW The wicked fairy in the Sleeping Beauty fairy tale represents the dark aspect of the Nornir. The spinning wheel on which Sleeping Beauty pricks her finger is a symbol of fate.

goodness. The Three Fates of Greek and Roman mythology were also spinners of the web of life. In Native American traditions, the spider is a symbol of fate.

DECIDERS OF FATE

Each of the goddesses played a distinct role. Urd (fate) was an old crone and represented the past. She could predict the future through her knowledge of past events and foretell people's fate based on their predispositions. Her sister Verdandi (being/existing) signified the present and was a stern taskmistress, demanding honesty, correctness, and responsibility. She made life difficult for those who were lazy, conceited, or undisciplined. The third sister Skuld (necessity) represented the future and saw to it that people learned from their mistakes. Her lessons helped people to progress along the path of life rather than stagnate.

ABOVE A painting by Henry Fuseli (1741–1825) showing the three Weird Sisters appearing to Macbeth and his companion Banquo in the Shakespeare tragedy *Macbeth*. The sisters symbolize fate and are representations of the Nornir.

READING
THE RUNES

Before you can start to use the runes, you
need to become familiar with their meanings.
This chapter considers each of the 24 runes of
the Elder Futhark, explaining their literal as
well as esoteric meanings. Some of the things
to which each rune corresponds, such as gods,
colors, and trees, are also listed.

1. fehu

The word fehu means cattle. cattle were the principal source of food and clothing to all the germanic peoples. Their horns also provided drinking cups, while their dung fertilized the land for crops.

A tribe or family's wealth and status were measured by the number of cattle they owned. The word *fehu* therefore also came to mean money or wealth and is the source of modern English words such as fee, fief, and feudal. On a more esoteric level, the Fehu rune concerns the true energetic nature of wealth, power, and success, both spiritually and materially.

ASSOCIATIONS

While possessions were valued by the Germanic peoples, the accumulation of individual wealth was frowned upon. The Anglo-Saxon Rune Poem says of Fehu: "Wealth is a comfort to everyone, yet each must give freely if he will glory in heaven." Fehu is sacred to Frey, lord of abundance, who represents generative male energy. His energy is expansive and animates all living things. This divine power is freely available in nature and should be shared for the common wealth, not to create divisions in status. Accumulated Fehu energy becomes stagnant when not allowed to circulate freely. It can then become poisonous and infect the miser who holds onto it for its own sake. Frey corresponds to the Hindu god Shiva. His energy is both creative and destructive, like electricity, and should be used wisely. Fehu's plant is the stinging nettle, which provides us with a clue about how to use Fehu's energy—the nettle does not sting if grasped firmly.

SHIVA

BELOW Cattle were the principal form of wealth for the Germanic peoples. Fehu, which means cattle, therefore represents wealth and status.

DIVINATORY MEANINGS

MUNDANE: Money, success, wealth, status, power
ESOTERIC: Generative energy, mobility, creativity, destruction

CORRESPONDENCES

PHONETIC VALUE: f
DEITY: Frey
TREE: Elder
PLANT: Stinging nettle
ANIMAL: Cat
BIRD: Swallow
ASTROLOGY: Aries
COLOR: Light red
ELEMENT: Fire

2. URUZ

Uruz means aurochs or urus, the mightily horned wild ox that roamed the forests of northern Europe for millennia until it was finally hunted to extinction during the seventeenth or eighteenth century.

ABOVE The aurochs or urus was an incredibly strong wild ox. The rune named after it therefore means strength.

These huge, untamable beasts were a byword for strength and ferocity. The Roman emperor Julius Caesar described them as being only slightly smaller than an elephant. Killing an aurochs was an important initiation rite for warriors, providing a fearsome challenge that required strength, courage, skill, and cunning.

ASSOCIATIONS
Phonetically, Uruz is the letter u, which is shaped like a pair of horns. Norse warriors attached horns to their helmets as totems capable of endowing them with the strength of the ox from which the horns were taken. The Germanic prefix *ur* means original or primitive. It represents the primal force

of life that alternates between the dual poles of
the masculine and the feminine. This primal force
is symbolized by horns, which are both phallic and
yonic, being hard and pointed but hollow inside. Uruz
is therefore both the vagina that receives the seed-generating
phallus and the phallus itself. Its shape also recalls
the cupped hand that molds and shapes the
clay of life. Horns were also believed by
the Germanic peoples to act as receivers
and transmitters of cosmic energy, like
radio antennae. Horned headdresses
were worn by Norse shamans to
tune into cosmic energies and
communicate with the gods. Uruz represents an
opportunity for spiritual advancement, the chance
to shape one's destiny, and to wield the primal
life force to powerful effect.

ABOVE **The horns on this
Viking helmet were meant
to impart the strength of
an ox to the wearer.**

SPHAGNUM MOSS

3. Thurisaz

This rune is called Thurisaz in the Germanic tongue and Thurs in old Norse, both of which mean giant, while the old English version, Thorn, means thorn as we understand it today.

DIVINATORY MEANINGS

MUNDANE: Obstacles, difficulties, protection, stubbornness, pride, vanity, heroic effort, patience, endurance

ESOTERIC: Opportunity to deflate the false ego, spiritual courage, protection of the sacred

CORRESPONDENCES

PHONETIC VALUE: th
DEITY: Thor
TREE: Blackthorn
PLANT: Briar/thistle/bramble
ANIMAL: Snake
BIRD: Albatross
ASTROLOGY: Mars
COLOR: Red
ELEMENT: Fire/earth

These variants share the same linguistic root as Thor, the god to whom the rune corresponds. Thurisaz looks like a thorn projecting from the stem of a bramble or wild rose, and means protection or obstacle, as in the old Germanic fairy tale of Sleeping Beauty, around whose castle a forest of thorns springs up. The forest acts as a formidable obstacle to any prince attempting to rescue her, preventing all but the most worthy from getting through.

THOR

ASSOCIATIONS

Thurisaz represents a barrier that cannot be easily surmounted. The walls of Norse fortifications often had projections built into them to prevent them from being scaled by enemies. Both thorns and giants act as obstacles to the vain and foolhardy. Thorns can deflate puffed-up pretensions with a bang, while giants can step on the unsuspecting whose eyes are not focused on higher things than themselves. Thurisaz suggests that an obstacle of considerable dimensions looms ahead or an inflated opinion of your own worthiness is impeding your progress.

Only courage or humility will help. In the former case, the only way to proceed is to retrace your steps and work around the problem, or to summon up a heroic effort worthy of the mighty Thor and fight your way through. In the latter case, you must face up to your own shortcomings with courage and honesty and humbly change your path. This self-evaluation will allow unlimited progress.

ABOVE Thurisaz looks like a thorn and represents both the obstacles and protection that thorns produce.

RIGHT Mars corresponds with Thurisaz, reflecting the rune's powerful and fiery strength.

4. ANSUZ

the germanic word ansuz means god, as does its old english equivalent ós, which also means mouth. The ansuz rune therefore means the mouth of a god, or that which issues from the mouth of a god.

DIVINATORY MEANINGS

MUNDANE: Advice, communication, contemplation, inspiration, authority, tradition, blessing

ESOTERIC: Initiation, divine inspiration

CORRESPONDENCES

PHONETIC VALUE: a
DEITY: Odin
TREE: Ash
PLANT: Fly agaric
ANIMAL: Wolf
BIRD: Raven
Astrology: Mercury
COLOR: Dark blue
ELEMENT: Air

The god in question here is Odin, the source of all the wisdom acquired by man. The Ansuz rune is the staff of Odin. The two sidebars on the staff represent the gifts given by Odin to Askr and Embla, the Adam and Eve of the Norse creation myth. These gifts were *anda* and *ódhr*. Anda is spirit, the breath of god that imparts life to all things. Ódhr is inspiration—literally, that which is breathed in. Ansuz is therefore both that which inspires and inspiration itself.

ASSOCIATIONS

The Old Norse equivalent of *ansuz* is *áss*. This word means god, specifically one of the Aesir, whose senior figure is Odin. It is the root of the word for ash tree. All trees were deemed sacred by the Germanic peoples, but preeminence was accorded to the ash because the world tree Yggdrasil was a giant ash. Yggdrasil's roots and branches embraced

RIGHT The psychoactive fly agaric mushroom was used by shamans to induce a trancelike state and is associated with Ansuz.

the nine worlds of the Germanic universe. This emphasizes the communication between the world of humans and other levels of reality that the Ansuz rune implies. The fly agaric mushroom is associated with Ansuz and was used by shamans to travel between the worlds. On a mundane level, Ansuz advises us to seek wise counsel and consider deeply before taking an important step. It can also represent the opportunity to receive or transmit a key piece of wisdom from the ancestral world soul.

ABOVE Ansuz means mouth of a god and corresponds with the ash tree, which was revered as the world tree Yggdrasil. It is specifically linked with Odin, god of wisdom and communication, and therefore symbolizes these attributes.

5. RAIDO

Raido means wagon and shares the same root as the old English words for ride and wheel (rad in German). It therefore has connotations of travel, journeying, and moving forward.

In Germanic mythology, the Sun was said to rest on a chariot that was pulled through the heavens by a horse. Raido represents both the wheel of time and a wheel pulled by a horse, symbolizing progress or process. The chief divinatory meaning of Raido is journey—both mundane travel and a sacred journey or spiritual quest.

ASSOCIATIONS

Wagon wheels were traditionally made of oak, the tree that corresponds to the Raido rune. Astrologically, the oak is ruled by the planet Jupiter. Personified by the Romans as a god, Jupiter was famous for his thunderbolts. The Germanic god of

thunder and lightning is Thor. The sound of thunder was said to be made by the wheels of his great chariot thundering across the skies. Raido, therefore, is sacred to Thor. The saying "stuck in a rut" harks back to the days of horse-drawn travel. If your wagon wheel becomes stuck in a rut, it takes a great effort to change direction and may require you to take a step into the unknown. By doing so,

you place your fate in the lap of the gods, who will guide you if you have sufficient faith to relinquish control. By allowing the universe to place new experiences in your path, you make yourself available for change to occur in your life. This can be a gradual process or it may be dramatic and sudden; as if struck by one of Thor's thunderbolts, your life can be transformed in a flash.

OPPOSITE Raido is sacred to Thor, the god of thunder and lightning, whose great chariot produced the noise of thunder as it raced through the skies.

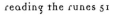

6. kenaz

In old German kenaz means torch, as does its Anglo-Saxon equivalent ken. The Old Norse for this rune is kaun, which has the meaning of sore, ulcer, or boil, while the Gothic is kusma, which translates as swelling.

DIVINATORY MEANINGS

MUNDANE: Knowledge, skill, controlled energy, successful idea, painful healing, sexual attraction
ESOTERIC: Spiritual illumination, inner guidance

CORRESPONDENCES

PHONETIC VALUE: k
DEITY: Wayland
TREE: Pine
PLANT: Mullein
ANIMAL: None
BIRD: Owl
ASTROLOGY: Venus
COLOR: Pink
ELEMENT: Fire/earth

The torch represents the use of fire to provide light in the darkness. The word ken is still current in Scotland and means to know. Knowledge is enlightenment. Boils and swellings are inflammations and eruptions of the skin, characterized by redness and heat. This use of inner fire is the body's way of ridding itself of toxins. Kenaz also shares the same root as the word cunning, which means craftiness, skill, or ingenuity— the use of knowledge to achieve specific results.

PINE

ASSOCIATIONS

The shape of the rune itself represents a directed beam of light. Kenaz is associated with the fire-working blacksmith Wayland or Wieland, the god of skills and crafts who used his forge to work metals and fashion precious jewelry. A word for an unworked gemstone is carbuncle, which

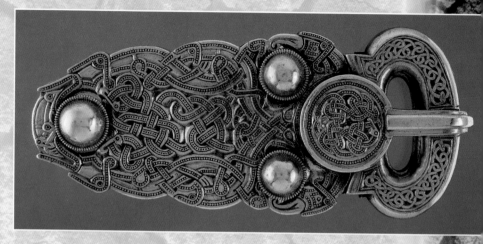

also has the meaning of a pustulent swelling. Kenaz can therefore signify the application of inner light or understanding in order to achieve your aims. This inner fire can be used to rid yourself of impurities and heal wounds, although this may involve some pain. There is also the suggestion that the misuse of knowledge can result in ulceration of the soul. Kenaz may denote that you are about to receive the gift of understanding or give this gift to another. The rune also has the connotation of knowing in the biblical sense, hence its astrological correspondence with Venus.

ABOVE A gold belt buckle from a seventh-century ship burial at Sutton Hoo, England. Kenaz is connected with crafts and is associated with the god Wayland, who fashioned precious jewelry.

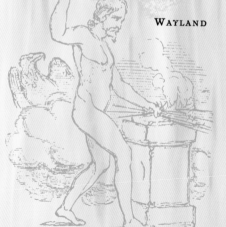

WAYLAND

VENUS

ABOVE & LEFT The Gebo rune can denote a significant partnership such as a marriage or business relationship. It may also indicate that you will receive a gift. This is not as straightforward as it seems, however, and involves making a pact to give something in exchange.

7. gebo

The word gebo means gift. It is derived from the same root as the modern English words gift and give. In the old Germanic traditions, the offering of a gift was not necessarily a straightforward affair.

ODIN

The recipient of a gift was always required to make a gift of equivalent value in return—"an eye for an eye, a tooth for a tooth." The god Odin gave one of his eyes to the divine sage Mimir in exchange for the gift of wisdom. He also had to offer himself in sacrifice on Yggdrasil in order to receive the runes. To ask for or accept a gift was therefore to agree to an exchange, to enter into a pact.

ASSOCIATIONS

On a divinatory level, this rune suggests that a gift has or will be offered by the gods. This may take the form of wisdom, insight, or an opportunity. However, the rune warns of the responsibilities inherent in accepting such a gift. The old Norse philosophy that "nothing comes from nothing" emphasizes the onus on the receiver of the gift to use it correctly. This sense of exchange or bond is echoed by the shape of the Gebo rune. It symbolizes a kiss and is used by millions every day when sending letters and messages of love. It is also the shape made in a blood brother pact, when the cut wrists of two people are crossed in a ritual exchange of blood. Gebo therefore also means mystical union and ritual partnership. On a more mundane level, it can signify the establishment of any partnership that is to play a significant part in your life.

DIVINATORY MEANINGS

MUNDANE: Gift, opportunity, love match, partnership, sacrifice, obligation
ESOTERIC: Karmic union

CORRESPONDENCES
PHONETIC VALUE: g
DEITY: Odin/Frigg
TREE: Ash/elm
PLANT: Wild pansy
ANIMAL: Ox
BIRD: None
ASTROLOGY: Pisces
COLOR: Deep blue
ELEMENT: Water

8. wunjo

wunjo is the joy rune.
The anglo-saxon rune poem
explains the runic meaning
of joy: "joy is needed not by those
who have little want and sorrow
and have increase and bliss."

DIVINATORY MEANINGS

MUNDANE: Joy, good news, celebration, success, reward, harmony, family, tribe, emotional release
ESOTERIC: Inner connectedness, spiritual well-being, universal family

CORRESPONDENCES

PHONETIC VALUE: w
DEITY: Frey
TREE: Ash
PLANT: Flax
ANIMAL: None
BIRD: None
ASTROLOGY: Leo
COLOR: Gold/yellow
ELEMENT: Fire/earth

In the poem a distinction is made between bliss and joy. Bliss is a serene happiness available only to those who have no hardships to contend with. Life was very tough in northern Europe a thousand years ago. Even kings and chieftains enjoyed less comfort than most of us now take for granted. Harvests often failed, and famine, disease, and warfare claimed their regular quota of victims. Joy is the reward for hope, patience, courage, and endurance. It is the celebration of a life worth fighting for.

ASSOCIATIONS

The Wunjo rune symbolizes a tribal flag. Joy is the glue that holds tribes and clans together. In ancient times, what made life worth the struggle was the sheer joy that people experienced when efforts were rewarded and they were able to celebrate moments of good fortune. When the tribes rejoiced together at the eight annual solar and fire festivals, tensions and enmities were dissolved in a communal sense of joy that confirmed their love and truth. Such rejoicing included a sense of gratitude that cares could be cast aside and hardships overcome. Wunjo's number is eight, which represents harmony, union, and the eternal cycles of nature. On a divinatory level, Wunjo can signify the arrival of good news and a period of happiness and well-being as a result of achieving balance in your life and harmony with others.

Wunjo represents the
times of joy and celebration
that unite families, friends,
and communities together.

9. Hagalaz

Hagalaz is generally considered to be one of the most ominous of the runes because its name means hail, one of the most destructive of all weather forms. However, it also bears the seeds of regeneration.

LILY OF THE VALLEY

DIVINATORY MEANINGS

MUNDANE: Misfortune, damage, shock, short-term distress followed by long-term rewards

ESOTERIC: Powerful natural forces, evolution, regeneration, cosmic union

CORRESPONDENCES

PHONETIC VALUE: h
DEITY: Ymir
TREE: Yew
PLANT: Lily of the valley
ANIMAL: None
BIRD: Goose
STONE: Aquamarine
ASTROLOGY: Uranus
COLOR: Ice blue
ELEMENT: Water/earth

In the Norse creation myth, the original being was the giant Ymir, who was born from melting ice. Frozen water was considered to contain the seed of life. In both the Anglo-Saxon and Icelandic rune poems, hail is referred to as a grain, signifying its life-bearing qualities. Falling as ice and melting slowly on the ground, hail releases its life-giving properties and allows the soil to absorb it. Heavy rain, by contrast, can cause flooding, running off the land before it can be absorbed and taking precious topsoil with it.

ASSOCIATIONS

The shape of the Hagalaz rune alludes to this transference of cosmic energy from one realm to the next. It is apparent that Hagalaz contains both destructive and creative aspects simultaneously. If unfortunately timed, Hagalaz may cause great damage and distress, but it contains within it the seeds of regeneration. The number nine represents knowledge; Odin hung for nine days and nights on Yggdrasil in order to perceive the runes. Nine signifies

birth or new beginnings, as represented by the human gestation period of nine moons. While eight represents a complete cycle, nine is the initial phase of a future cycle. The Nordic universe consists of nine worlds, so nine also symbolizes totality. Hagalaz therefore signifies the end of one cycle and the beginning of a new one. This will be a difficult time, but the challenges you face will make you stronger and herald a positive and rewarding transformation.

ABOVE Hagalaz means hail. Representing powerful natural forces, it signifies misfortune and damage but also bears the seeds of regeneration.

ABOVE Nineteenth-century engraving of Old Father
Time, one of the manifestations of Saturn. He is a hard
taskmaster who demands that you pay your dues.

10. Naudhiz

The tenth rune goes by the name of Nyd in Old English and Nauths in Gothic. It translates as need, necessity, and distress. Naudhiz warns us to consider our deepest needs but to guard against compulsive desires.

Humans are frail creatures, whose bodies and souls need constant care, warmth, and nourishment. Of all the creatures under the Sun, humans are the only ones who may need to clothe themselves in order to survive. This was particularly true for the tribes living in cold northern climates, who had to learn skills such as hunting and weaving in order to clothe their bodies.

ASSOCIATIONS

Naudhiz is governed by the constellation of Capricorn, which reigns during midwinter and is ruled by Saturn, the planet of severity and restriction. The shape of the Naudhiz rune represents the tools used for kindling fire: the upright bore and the bow that turns it. Mastery of fire was a vital skill in surviving harsh winters. Naudhiz is therefore the mother of invention, the compulsion that forces us to work in order to survive and evolve. In order to become a free spirit, however, we must decide what is worthy of our efforts. The limitations of material comforts must be recognized in order for the soul to find deeper nourishment. The needs of the soul are ultimately more compelling than those of the body, because the soul can become immortal while the body is doomed to die. Greed withers the soul; luxury weakens it.

SATURN

II. ISA

Isa has the same meaning in all the old Germanic tongues: ice. Ice represents stasis, the ceasing of all flow, the arresting of all movement. Isa therefore suggests obstacles and hindrance.

Ice puts a freeze on all plans and imposes stillness. This is not generally considered desirable, but a verse from the Anglo-Saxon Rune Poem provides some perspective: "Ice is cold and slippery; it glistens like glass, is as bright as gems; the field wrought with frost is fair to the sight." Ice may be tedious or even dangerous, but it is beautiful nevertheless.

ASSOCIATIONS

The shape of the Isa rune symbolizes both an icicle and the capital letter I, which represents the higher self of the individual. The number 11 signifies a narrow gateway through which the self-contained individual can pass if still and fine enough; thus, inner progress can be achieved through stillness. The message is that, if you find your path blocked and your plans temporarily frustrated, you might benefit from appreciating the stillness. The sound of silence is exhilarating, particularly when discovered for the first time. It creates space and a greater sense

DIVINATORY MEANINGS

MUNDANE: Stasis, frustration of plans, obstacles, imposed rest, stillness
ESOTERIC: Inner stillness, initiation, appreciation of the present, acceptance, surrender

CORRESPONDENCES

PHONETIC VALUE: i
DEITY: Verdandi
TREE: Alder
PLANT: Henbane
ANIMAL: Reindeer
BIRD: Snowy owl
ASTROLOGY: Moon
COLOR: Black
ELEMENT: Earth

of presence. The universe seems more immediate, more imbued with meaning and resonance precisely because the heedless whirl of mundane events seems to have been stilled for a moment. When confronted with the Isa rune, the wisest course of action is to surrender to the will of the universe. There is much to be gained from a period of introspection.

ABOVE Isa means ice and stillness and is connected with the number 11, which represents a gateway through which you can pass once you have achieved inner stillness.

Jera promises a plentiful harvest and a time of abundance as long as you live your life in accordance with natural law.

12. Jera

The number 12 signifies the solar cycle of 12 months. Appropriately, it is also the number of Jera, the rune whose name means year, the full solar cycle. In the old Germanic tongue, jera also means harvest.

These meanings provide the rune's traditional divinatory interpretation. It signifies the completion of a process and the rewards that follow if you have acted correctly. This means correct in a natural rather than an ethical sense, since this rune is concerned with natural law rather than human convention. In other words, if you act in accordance with nature's laws, by gathering seed correctly and planting it at the right time in well-prepared soil, then with luck and good weather you can expect to harvest a full crop. Correct action reaps its own rewards in the fullness of time.

ASSOCIATIONS
The shape of the Jera rune suggests motion. This is the dynamism produced by the interaction of heavenly and earthly forces. The inherent dualism of Jera suggests the inner turmoil that results from wrong action or inaction. The message may be that you need to realign with the natural order of things. This could involve suffering. There is no such thing as a free lunch—you have to earn your daily bread in a way that does not go against the grain of life. You must sow the seed for next year's bread or you cannot expect a harvest and will suffer the pangs of starvation. Those who live their lives in accordance with natural law can expect to be rewarded for their efforts.

13. Eihwaz

Eihwaz means yew tree, one of the most revered trees among the northern European peoples and considered by some scholars to be the symbol for the world tree Yggdrasil rather than the ash.

MUNDANE: Flexibility, endurance, protection, change, empowerment, problem solving

ESOTERIC: Magical empowerment, psychic protection, spiritual attainment

CORRESPONDENCES

PHONETIC VALUE: Somewhere between e and i; seldom used in writing

DEITY: Odin

TREE: Yew

PLANT: Mandrake

ANIMAL: Hedgehog

BIRD: Heron

ASTROLOGY: Scorpio

COLOR: Black

ELEMENT: Earth

The yew is probably the longest-living tree in Europe. The Druids considered the yew to be an emblem of immortality because of this longevity, which is enhanced by the tree's flexibility and fast-rootedness that make it invulnerable to storms.

ASSOCIATIONS

The strong, flexible, close-grained wood of the yew was used to make the best longbows. This weapon was effective for both hunting prey and as a defense against enemies. The yew therefore both sustains and defends life as well as wields death. This ambivalence is reflected by the number of the Eihwaz rune: 13. Similarly, although most parts of the yew are toxic, the tree has recently been found to contain a highly effective anticancer agent. The shape of the rune also demonstrates this ambivalence. It points up, down, and to both sides. It represents a hook that can capture and bind. Eihwaz is therefore a powerful tool in the hands of those who can aim carefully. It is a magic wand that gives power over life and death. Eihwaz can sometimes indicate symbolic death, such as the end of a relationship, but more often it is a sign of empowerment, frequently of a mystical nature.

Eihwaz means yew. The yew is
one of only two trees that has
a rune named after it.

14. pertho

pertho is the most difficult to interpret of all the runes because even its mundane meaning is uncertain. It has been translated variously as apple tree, pear tree, chess piece, dice cup, fate, game, dance, hearth, and vagina.

DIVINATORY MEANINGS

MUNDANE: Mystery, chance, unpredictable event, sexual encounter, faults or mistakes exposed
ESOTERIC: Feminine mysteries, unfolding of fate, karma, initiatory event, incubation

CORRESPONDENCES
PHONETIC VALUE: p
DEITY: Nornir
TREE: Elm
PLANT: Belladonna
ANIMAL: Woman
BIRD: Heron
ASTROLOGY: Saturn
COLOR: Black
ELEMENT: Water

Since its meaning has remained a mystery or secret for so long, it seems appropriate to accept Pertho as the rune of mystery. Every runemaster who progresses along the path of knowledge will find particular significance in this rune and will invest it with meanings that are likely to alter as deeper levels of mystical insight are attained.

ASSOCIATIONS

The shape of the Pertho rune represents a container standing on its side. All vessels are symbols of the feminine principle, which is the matrix that contains the potential of all things. Inside they are dark and secretive, their contents mysterious. Pertho resembles a cauldron turned on its side and emptied of its contents. The cauldron is a familiar symbol in Germanic myth and fairy tales and is associated with witchcraft, magic potions, and feminine wisdom. The cauldron represents the Nordic concept of *orlog*, which can be compared with the Hindu and Buddhist law of karma. The cauldron itself is not fate or destiny, but it is the vessel within which they are brewed. To the uninitiated, fate is a matter of chance in which they play no active part, hence the association of Pertho with a dice cup and games of chance. However, the fact is that all of your thoughts and actions are stirred into the cauldron by your own hand as you unwittingly brew your own fate.

Pertho looks like a cauldron
lying on its sides. Cauldrons are
associated with magic, feminine
wisdom, and mystery.

ABOVE The tenth-century Jelling Stone from Denmark depicts a Christ figure standing in the Algiz pose with a runic inscription beneath. This restoration shows how the stone would originally have been painted with bright colors.

15. Algiz

Algiz has been translated as elk, protection, swan, and sedge grass. The gothic word alhs, meaning sanctuary or temple, may come from the same linguistic root.

DIVINATORY MEANINGS

MUNDANE: Protection, sanctuary, prayer, friendship, trust

ESOTERIC: Mystical communication with the divine, guardian spirit, absorption of protective cosmic energy, faith in the divine

CORRESPONDENCES

PHONETIC VALUE: z
DEITY: Heimdall
TREE: Yew
PLANT: Angelica
ANIMAL: Elk
BIRD: Dove
ASTROLOGY: Virgo
COLOR: Gold
ELEMENT: Earth/air

The Algiz rune was often used by warriors as a symbol of protection and this seems to be its principal function. Raising the hand palm forward with the middle three fingers splayed was an old Germanic sign of protection against evil and this also recalls the rune's shape.

ASSOCIATIONS

The shape of the rune could represent many things, such as a tree, a raised hand, an elk's antlers, a swan in flight, or a person standing with raised arms. When appealing to the gods, it was customary among pagan peoples to stand with arms raised toward heaven. This action draws down divine energy from above. In this context, Algiz is the rune that links humans with the gods. For this reason the rune is considered sacred to Heimdall, the god who guarded the rainbow bridge that linked the realm of the gods with the realm of humankind. Heimdall, whose name means "he who casts bright rays," is the protector of both gods and men. He is traditionally depicted wielding a mighty sword and it was Heimdall who killed the trickster god Loki during the titanic last battle known as the Twilight of the Gods. The Algiz rune suggests that protection may be needed, but confirms that such protection is assured. All you need to do is confirm your link with the divine through prayer.

HEIMDALL

16. sowilu

Also known as sigil in old English and sol in old Norse, sowilu is the sun rune. The sun is a principal focus of worship in all pagan religions, and even in christianity, jesus is linked to the sun in his role as the Light of god.

The Sun is the heavenly body on which all life depends. It is therefore a symbol of the light of creation itself. Although the Sun is widely considered to be a symbol of the active masculine principle, among the Germanic peoples it was originally considered feminine, being the goddess Sonne, while the Moon was considered masculine. The Sun symbolizes consciousness, vitality, fertility, life force, the will, and the desire to be.

ASSOCIATIONS

The solar god of the Nordic pantheon was the Christlike Baldur, the innocent god of love, light, and beauty. Plants that correspond to Sowilu include mistletoe, a dart of which killed Baldur, and chamomile, known to the Norse people as "Baldur's brow," its flower being a yellow solar disk with an aura of bright white petals. Sowilu is entirely positive as an individual rune, confirming that all is well. When accompanied by more difficult runes, however, it may suggest overconfidence. When dazzled by your own prospects or desires, you can become blind to other factors in your life. When entering even a normally lit room from the bright outdoors, it can appear dark. In such circumstances, you should pause to allow your vision to adjust rather than risk stumbling. The rune may also warn you not to outshine others too brazenly or you could cause offense or inspire jealousy.

OPPOSITE Sowilu represents the positive energy of the Sun. This Scandinavian stone features a stylized runic symbol of solar power.

MISTLETOE

DIVINATORY MEANINGS

MUNDANE: Success, vitality, good fortune, popularity
ESOTERIC: The higher self, the spiritual will, enlightenment, divine blessing

CORRESPONDENCES
PHONETIC VALUE: s
DEITY: Baldur/Sonne
TREE: Juniper
PLANT: Chamomile/mistletoe
ANIMAL: Lion
BIRD: Eagle
ASTROLOGY: Sun
COLOR: Yellow
ELEMENT: Fire

17. Teiwaz

Teiwaz was the original creator god of the Germanic peoples, who later became known as Tyr. His name is related to the Sanskrit word dyaus, meaning divine, and to Jehovah, a Hebrew name for god.

DIVINATORY MEANINGS

MUNDANE: Victory, honor, justice, law, balance, self-sacrifice, righteousness
ESOTERIC: Magical equilibrium, selflessness, spiritual purity

CORRESPONDENCES

PHONETIC VALUE: t
DEITY: Tyr
TREE: Oak
PLANT: Wolfsbane
ANIMAL: Wolf
BIRD: Crow
ASTROLOGY: Libra
COLOR: Red
ELEMENT: Air

ABOVE Teiwaz is the rune of the god Tyr and denotes self-sacrifice. Tyr sacrificed his hand, which was bitten off by the great wolf Fenrir, to protect the other gods.

OAK

As the exploits of the anthropomorphic hero gods such as Odin and Thor became elaborated in myth, so the importance of Teiwaz diminished. Eventually, he became simply one of the Aesir and was generally referred to by the name of Tyr. Tyr's new role was that of a law god who presided over assemblies and whose special concern was justice in war. Warriors would call upon him to grant them the courage and righteousness needed to secure victory.

ABOVE Tyr's special concern was military justice. He was often depicted carrying a spear, which echoes the shape of the Teiwaz rune.

ASSOCIATIONS

Tyr's name is recalled, obliviously by most, every time the day of the week dedicated to him is mentioned: Tuesday. As a model of masculine honor and courage, Tyr corresponds to the positive aspects of the Roman god Mars, whose day of the week he shares (*Martis dies* in Latin; *Mardi* in French). The shape of the Teiwaz rune represents a spear, arrow, or military rod of justice. Like the astrological symbol for Mars, which it also resembles, Tyr is a phallic emblem of masculine procreative energy. It may also be seen as the central axis between the eternally conflicting yet complementary polarities in nature: masculine/feminine, light/dark, creative/destructive. The *Eddas* describe Tyr's most famous exploit when his right hand was bitten off by the great wolf Fenrir in a selfless act of sacrifice to protect the gods. Teiwaz is therefore a rune of self-sacrifice, justice, and military honor. It indicates that the truth will be victorious, justice will prevail, and heralds a time of success, although this may involve a selfless act or sacrifice of some kind.

18. berkana

berkana, or beorc in old english, means birch tree. this graceful tree has the poetic name lady of the woods and is probably the only tree to be found throughout the entire area peopled by germanic tribes.

LEFT Berkana is associated with May Day. The Germanic peoples dedicated May Eve to the Moon goddess Walpurga. Here, a witch in fantastical costume leaps over a bonfire during Walpurgisnacht celebrations in Germany.

Berkana means birch tree and is associated with fertility. The ancient Germanic peoples sometimes used birch twigs to flagellate the body in order to promote fertility.

Coppiced birch produces tall, straight poles and was often used as the maypole during May Day fertility rites. The Germanic peoples dedicated this festival to the Moon goddess Walpurga, and in Germany May Eve is still called Walpurgisnacht. Despite the phallic connotations of the maypole, Berkana is essentially a symbol of feminine fertility and the mother principle. The flexible twigs of the birch were formerly used for light flagellation in a treatment believed to promote fertility.

ASSOCIATIONS

The shape of the rune clearly represents a woman's breasts. The symbol of Berkana's corresponding astrological sign Cancer also depicts a cradled pair of breasts. Berkana is therefore associated with new beginnings or fresh projects that require careful nurturing to ensure that they achieve fruition. Products derived from the birch emphasize Berkana's beneficial attributes. They include oil of birch tar, which helps to preserve leather and has a beautifying effect on the skin. Birch wine, made from fermented sap, is a good tonic. Berkana is clearly an auspicious rune, but in some circumstances may indicate that greater care should be taken.

19. Ehwaz

Ehwaz means horse in all the old Germanic tongues. In some respects, the horse came to be an even more important animal to the Indo-European peoples than cattle.

DIVINATORY MEANINGS

MUNDANE: Travel, partnership, marriage, self-control
ESOTERIC: Inner journeys, astral projection

CORRESPONDENCES

PHONETIC VALUE: e
DEITY: Odin
TREE: Ash
PLANT: Ragwort
ANIMAL: Horse
BIRD: Albatross
ASTROLOGY: Gemini
COLOR: White/yellow
ELEMENT: Air

Indeed, without the special relationship established between human and horse, the herding and domestication of cattle would not have been possible. Moreover, the survival of tribal groups, in the face of competition from aggressive neighbors, depended on their horse mastery and the number of horses they could breed or capture.

ASSOCIATIONS

The Norse myths tell of the greatness of Sleipnir, the eight-legged white stallion of Odin. Sleipnir was the strongest and swiftest horse ever to exist, to whom no obstacle was insurmountable. The horse provided humans with the power to cover great distances, sweep down upon enemies, and hunt swift prey. True horsemanship is a great accomplishment. Breaking in a wild horse requires more than brute force; the cooperation of the horse is required. A relationship has to be established that is based on mutual trust. Although Ehwaz implies travel, it also refers to the progress that can be made through cooperation. The shape of the rune suggests the reins and bit with which the horse is controlled and directed. The master of this rune stands head to head with his or her own dual nature. It signifies the control of will, the direction of energy, and the wisdom of cooperation between the two.

OPPOSITE Ehwaz means horse and symbolizes self-control and both physical and spiritual journeys.

ASH

ABOVE Eighth-century Viking stone depicting Odin riding his eight-legged horse Sleipnir and the Valkyries guarding the gates of Valhalla.

20. Mannaz

Mannaz translates as human and represents the mystery of each human being's relationship with other humans, the rest of creation, and the divine will.

As human beings we are all involved in a series of unfolding mysteries. The most immediate is our own story, the pursuit of our own personal destiny. Next comes the story of the family, group, or tribe to which we belong. Finally, we are all connected through these relationships to the fundamental riddles of life. The fate of the universe, of the divine itself, resides in the soul of every individual.

Associations

Like its individual members, the human race is more or less consciously pursuing its destiny, which in turn is bound up with the destiny of the Earth, the universe, and the divine plan itself. The Mannaz rune is shaped like two mirror-image banners or flags. Humankind's destiny is shown to be attached not just to the tribal banner, but also to the banner of creation itself, of which humans are a reflection. Your consciousness is limited only by your sense of identity. A narrow sense of identity can separate you from others. As you transcend gender, tribal, and national identification, you become more conscious. When you embrace the universe wholeheartedly, you are universally conscious. Mannaz represents the mystery of this most fundamental relationship: the microcosm of humankind and the macrocosm of the universe. It represents the transcendent, androgynous, divinely conscious human.

DIVINATORY MEANINGS

MUNDANE: The self, family member, friendship, association, rational intelligence, race memory

ESOTERIC: Transcendental consciousness, the individual as microcosm, shaman, spiritual healer

CORRESPONDENCES

PHONETIC VALUE: m
DEITY: Heimdall
TREE: Holly
PLANT: Mandrake
ANIMAL: Man
BIRD: Hawk
ASTROLOGY: Aquarius
COLOR: Red
ELEMENT: Water/air

Mannaz means human and represents individual consciousness and the relationship of each human being with other humans as well as the universe.

21. LAGUZ

Laguz means body of water, sea, or ocean and is the root of the modern English word lake. The rune looks like the carved prow of a viking longship and represents a vehicle used to navigate water.

The Germanic peoples believed that at death the soul journeyed across the waters to the underworld. This is why the Vikings favored ship burials. Great warriors and chieftains were immolated in a blazing longship pushed out to sea to symbolize the soul's final journey. At birth, children were sprinkled with water to initiate them into clan membership in a ritual similar to the Christian practice of baptism.

ASSOCIATIONS

NJÖRD

Water is the matrix of life, the womb from which all the creatures on Earth have emerged. Although all surface life is sustained by sunlight and water, in the depths of the oceans, where there is no light at all, it is water alone that sustains. Water is magnetic, receptive, and conductive. It is ruled, in its tides and rhythms, by the Moon, whose monthly cycles have a direct influence on all living things. The human vehicles of response to the watery and lunar aspects of life are the emotions, dreams, and intuition—the passive side of the

psyche. These vehicles define our sensitivity, allowing us to explore our deepest feelings. This process of exploration, in turn, nurtures and develops the soul, which is the supreme vehicle of individual consciousness. On an esoteric level, the Lagaz rune may indicate a great journey of the soul that could involve an immersion into the deep primordial waters. Pain and struggle may precede the soul's reemergence into the light.

BELOW The dragon-headed prow of a Viking longship. The Laguz rune is shaped like a prow and represents a journey across water.

ABOVE The Moon rules the tides and rhythms of water. Laguz, which means body of water, is therefore connected with the lunar attributes of emotions and intuition.

22. INGWAZ

This rune is dedicated to the mysterious god Ing, whose origins are unclear. He is generally believed to predate the Germanic tribes and became associated with the fertility god Frey.

Despite the lack of record about Ing, scholars broadly agree on the significance of his rune. The rune is usually described as a phallic symbol representing the head of a penis, but it could just as easily represent a womb or vagina. Ingwaz therefore represents potency and sexual energy.

FREY

ASSOCIATIONS

Ingwaz is the magnetic charge that draws the polarities together, attracting male to female and female to male. This energy is expressed in both sexes as an inner heat, the heat of procreative sexual desire. It generates the physical and psychic responses necessary for the procreative sexual act. The latent energy of Ingwaz builds to the point of orgasm, whereupon it is released. Ingwaz is goal driven; its objective is fruition. Once its charge is spent, Ingwaz gestates in the seeds that it has engendered, its energy rebuilding to the point where it reemerges as the latent potency in a new being, whether plant or animal. This mystery was acted

The Ring of Brodgar in the Orkney Islands, Scotland. Phallic symbols such as standing stones and the Ingwaz rune can signify both sexual energy and intense creative activity.

DIVINATORY MEANINGS

MUNDANE: Potency, latent energy, sexual heat, orgasm, union, fruition, goal
ESOTERIC: Intense creative activity

CORRESPONDENCES
PHONETIC VALUE: ng
DEITY: Ing/Frey
TREE: Apple
PLANT: Self-heal
ANIMAL: Boar
BIRD: Cuckoo
ASTROLOGY: Black moon
COLOR: Orange
ELEMENT: Fire

out in the pagan harvest festivals of the north European peoples. One such rite involved the actual beheading of the erect penis of a selected Harvest King at the moment of orgasm. The gush of blood and semen spilled on the soil of a harvested field would ensure the next year's fertility through its potent charge of Ingwaz energy. Ingwaz therefore represents the "little death" of orgasm that engenders new life and denotes creative energy, union, and completion.

OPPOSITE & RIGHT Ingwaz represents magnetic sexual attraction and orgasm. Pagan harvest rites acted out the release of sexual energy and the spilling of seed to encourage a bountiful harvest.

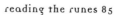

23. othila

othila means homeland or
ancestral property. it contains a
sense of homecoming and returning
to one's roots and represents
appreciation for and reconciliation
with the ancestral spirits.

Othila means homeland and
symbolizes the powers of insight
that can be attained by honoring
ancient traditions and connecting
with ancestral spirits.

The archetypal story of the hero setting out to seek his fortune and returning to find that the treasure was at home all along is tied up with the significance of Othila. Some rune scholars place Othila at the end of the rune-row because of this meaning of homecoming, but it makes more sense to place the Dagaz rune in that position because it represents endings and new beginnings.

ASSOCIATIONS

Most adolescents rebel in one manner or another. Driven by a need to establish their own identity, they break free of their home ties and head off to see what life has in store for them. However, life has a habit of bringing things full circle. As they mature, they often discover that much of what they had been in conflict with can actually be embraced with respect and understanding. It is not a regression to return to an originating point. It is a sign of deeper involvement in the great evolutionary spiral. Happiness and fulfillment are found not just through achievements, but also by identifying with universal truths. By honoring the fundamental truths enshrined in ancient tradition, we can tap into the integral power of the tribe. This process is timeless and universal, being the way of all peoples. The ancient runemasters understood that they could have access to great powers of insight by connecting with the ancestor spirits. Othila therefore represents both physical property and this secret inheritance, the true power in the land.

DIVINATORY MEANINGS

MUNDANE: Homeland, ancestral property, family home, inheritance
ESOTERIC: Ancestor spirits, sacred enclosure, universal truth

CORRESPONDENCES
PHONETIC VALUE: o
DEITY: Odin
TREE: Hawthorn
PLANT: Daisy
ANIMAL: Salmon
BIRD: Raven
ASTROLOGY: Moon
COLOR: Yellow
ELEMENT: Fire

24. DAGAZ

Dagaz means day and signifies both beginnings and endings. The shape of the rune is an angular form of the lemniscate, the horizontal figure eight that symbolizes eternity.

DIVINATORY MEANINGS

MUNDANE: Security, certainty, clarity, dramatic change
ESOTERIC: Higher level of consciousness, path of destiny

CORRESPONDENCES

PHONETIC VALUE: d
DEITY: Oestre/Verdandi
TREE: Rowan
PLANT: Clary sage
ANIMAL: Deer
BIRD: Skylark
ASTROLOGY: Half moon
COLOR: Light blue
ELEMENT: Air

The Dagaz rune represents the endlessly repeating cycles of time, such as the flow of day into night and night into day, or summer falling into winter and springing back again. The central point of the rune where the mirrored opposites connect is the kiss of the Sun as it banishes the night, flooding the darkness and initiating the day.

ASSOCIATIONS

The long, cold nights made winter in the Nordic lands a grueling ordeal. In Scandinavia, midwinter was an endless night, with the Sun staying below the horizon for days before beginning the slow climb back to its midsummer zenith. The shape of the Dagaz rune symbolizes the spring and fall equinoxes, when night and day are of equal length. These occur around March 21st and September 21st. Although the rune's shape gives equal weight to both light and dark, in fact Dagaz emphasizes the light of the Sun because it is the light that defines the darkness. Dagaz represents the dawn of the spring equinox and the

start of a new cycle of growth. The rune is sacred to Oestre or Ostara, the goddess of the dawn and spring, who gives us the words Easter and estrogen, the female fertility hormone. Dagaz also symbolizes the eternal light that is latent even in the depths of darkness. The seeking and nourishing of this inner light sustains the spiritual warrior in the darkness and provides us with the heart to endure and await the new dawn.

ABOVE Dagaz means day and signifies beginnings and endings. Its main emphasis, however, is on the light of the Sun and the promise of the new dawn.

OPPOSITE A solar eclipse illustrates the meaning of Dagaz. Although the passing Moon produces a period of darkness, it is the aura of the Sun that gives the darkness definition.

CLARY SAGE

MAKING &
CASTING
RUNESTONES

Although runestones can be bought commercially, most runemasters fashion a personal set of runes. Traditionally, this should not be attempted until a high degree of familiarity with the runes has been achieved. All that is truly needed, however, is an open mind and a humble attitude.

choosing the material

when you are ready to make a set of runestones, the first thing you need to consider is what type of material to use. earth, wood, stones, and bones can all be successfully worked to make runestones.

In fact, you can make runestones from almost any material, even glass or metal. Nothing is forbidden or considered wrong, but the matter should be given serious consideration. Factors to bear in mind include size, weight, durability, workability, and availability.

WOOD

Given the name, you might think that stones would be the most authentic material, but actually it is wood that is most commonly used. It is considered traditional to use the wood of a fruit-bearing tree, because this is mentioned by the Roman historian Tacitus in his monograph about the Germanic peoples (*Germania*, chapter 10). This does not just refer to trees that produce dessert fruit, however. Most trees, including oak, hawthorn, and yew, produce fruits of some kind. In many ways, wood is the ideal option. As well as being sacred to the Germanic peoples, wood is comparatively light, durable, and easy to carve. It also has the advantage of being readily available from a living source, even in the heart of a major metropolis.

ALTERNATIVE MATERIALS

Clay from the earth can also be shaped and fired to make runestones. This is relatively easy to do with a little pottery-making knowledge, and many commercial sets are made from clay. Pebbles and stones are also sometimes used, but they can be hard to carve. Although you can paint the symbols on the stones, the paint can chip or fade and the process of physically impressing the rune glyphs is omitted.

The Vikings often carved runes from bone, particularly whalebone. Deer antler can also be used, especially the tines.

ABOVE Runestones can easily be carved from deer antlers if you have access to this material.

ABOVE & OPPOSITE You can use any type of material to make runestones, including clay, stones, bone, glass, and metal. Wood is the most traditional material and almost any type of tree would be suitable.

making & casting runestones 93

selecting a Tree

To make a set of runestones from wood, you must first select a living tree. There are many fine candidates to choose from, especially those that correspond to the runes themselves.

ABOVE The silver birch could be found throughout the Germanic lands and has a rune, Berkana, named after it.

Two trees have a rune specifically named after them. One is the yew, which gives its name to the rune Eihwaz. This long-lived hardwood has a natural red color, which is the traditional color of runestones. The other tree rune is Berkana, which is named after the beautiful silver birch. Its wood is relatively soft, however, so runestones made from silver birch may be less durable.

ASH AND ELM
Ash and elm trees are excellent choices because they equate with Askr and Embla, the original couple from whom all human beings are descended. According to the *Song of the Sybil*, when the earth was young, Odin and his two brothers Vili and Ve found an ash and an elm tree. The trees were weak and feeble, with no fate assigned to them. They had no breath, blood, senses, language, or life hue.

EMBLA & ASKR

LEFT Sacred to Thor, the oak tree is fine grained and produces attractive and durable runestones.

Odin gave them breath. Vili gave them senses. Blood and life hue were given by Ve. This life-giving ritual is re-created when you carve, color, and energize your runestones. The ash also has the honor of being associated with the world tree Yggdrasil. It is easy to work and has a fine, pale wood that stains well. The elm produces a wonderful hard wood. Unfortunately, it is now very rare in some parts of the world, due to the ravages of disease.

OAK AND HAWTHORN

The oak is sacred to Thor and is prized by woodworkers for its fine-grained quality and durability. Another popular choice is the hawthorn, one of a trinity of sacred fairy trees together with the oak and ash. The blood-red fruit of the hawthorn is one of nature's finest heart medicines. Its wood is admirably tough. The most important factor when choosing a tree, however, is that it should particularly appeal to you.

RIGHT Revered for the medicinal properties of its fruits, the hawthorn is a good choice for making runestones.

preparing the wood

It is best to cut wood for making runestones just before the tree comes into leaf or blossom. An ideal time is spring equinox, when the latent energy that has built up during winter is about to burst forth.

ABOVE Cut a 2-foot (60-cm) long branch that is approximately 1–2 inches (2–5 cm) in diameter to make a set of runestones.

Spring equinox occurs around March 21st in the Northern Hemisphere and September 21st in the Southern Hemisphere. You will need a branch that is about 2 feet (60 cm) long. It does not have to be any thicker than 1–2 inches (2–5 cm) in diameter.

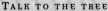

TALK TO THE TREE

Find your tree and establish a rapport with it. Do not be shy—talk to it; touch it. It will not know your language, but it will feel your nature and intent. Tell it what you have in mind and persuade it to give you a small branch freely for your sacred purpose. Bring the tree offerings in exchange, such as tobacco, silver, compost, or blood. At the appropriate time, take the branch in your nonwriting hand and give the tree a moment to withdraw its energy. Cut the

branch as swiftly as possible with the sharp blade of a saw or
knife. An old-fashioned billhook is ideal and will cut through a
2-inch (5-cm) branch in a single stroke. Pruning shears can also
be used. Never try to break a branch with your hands. Once cut,
rub some mud into the stump on the tree to salve it.

ABOVE Leave an offering
of tobacco, silver, or
compost at the base of the
tree as thanks for the
wood you have cut.

SEASON THE WOOD

Trim the branch to the required length and remove any side twigs or thorns. Cut a vertical
slit along the length of the branch, just deep enough so that you can peel off the bark.
Season the wood by leaving the peeled branch in a warm, dry place such as a linen closet
for at least three months. For harder woods, such as oak, hawthorn, and yew, a year is better.

OPPOSITE Establish a rapport
with the tree you are cutting
the wood from by talking to it.
You might like to do this at
dawn or dusk when you are
less likely to be disturbed.

fashioning the stones

The making of runestones re-creates the life-giving ritual of Askr and Embla, the ash and elm trees from which Odin and his brothers created the first human beings. Runes are living things. When you make runes, you create life.

By carving the rune, you give it senses (shape). By coloring it, you give it the hue of life. By chanting its name, you give it breath (energy). Each rune has its own energy, and the more attuned you are to that energy, the better the runestones will be charged.

CARVING THE RUNES
Saw the seasoned branch into slices. The finished stones need be no more than ¼ inch (5 mm) thick, but always cut the slices a little thicker to allow for sanding. Sand them as smooth as you wish, then inscribe the rune glyphs with a sharp chisel or knife. Alternately, brand them using a heated, flat-ended screwdriver or a soldering iron.

COLORING THE RUNES
Runes may be stained with their corresponding colors by steeping them in vegetable dyes. Traditionally, however, they are colored red. You can steep them in red wine to do this or use your own blood; there is no doubt that blood connects the runes powerfully to their maker. To do this, dip a sharp stick in blood drawn from a finger or thumb and rub it into the grooves you have carved into the wood; there is no need to steep the stones in blood.

ENERGIZING THE RUNES
To charge each rune, chant its name and meanings while you are carving and coloring it. This is best achieved by composing alliterative chants. For example, while fashioning the Raido rune, make up a chant using words such as ride, radial, ritual, radiate, roll, round, right, rite, rut, and rhythm. All of these words start with the phonetic "r" sound and are resonant in meaning with the Raido rune.

OPPOSITE Use wood-carving tools to inscribe the rune glyphs, then color them with red wine or blood.

Runic Divination

Divination is the magical art of discovering hidden things, foreseeing future events, or discerning the likely outcome of current situations. It is the most popular way of using the runes.

There is no record of the precise ways in which ancient runemasters used the runes for divinatory purposes, so modern runemasters tend to adapt the methods used in other divinatory systems, such as the tarot. Usually, a specific number of runes are selected randomly, laid into set positions, and then interpreted. The different formats in which the runes are laid are known as runecasts or spreads (see pages 104–109).

USING A RUNE POUCH

Before you begin runecasting, you should make a pouch in which to store your runes. A rune pouch should be sufficiently large to allow the runestones to become thoroughly mixed when shaken. Some runecasters like to draw the runestones directly from the shaken pouch and place them in the appropriate position of the runecast. Others prefer to cast all of the runes onto a special cloth, usually black linen, silk, or velvet, and then turn all of the runestones face up and consider each one briefly. Afterward, they turn the runes face down, swirl them around, and select the required number of runes for the runecast. Some people like to select the runes with their left hand, which is governed by the feminine, intuitive, and receptive aspect of our nature. Sensitive people may even feel a magnetic pull that draws their hand to a particular rune.

ASKING A QUESTION

It is usual, although not essential, to ask a specific question before carrying out a runecast. If you are performing a runecast for someone else, this person is usually referred to as the querent—the person who is asking the question. When formulating a question, keep it simple and direct.

OPPOSITE Keep your runestones in a pouch and, if you wish, perform runecasts on a special cloth.

Reversed Runes

2. URUZ *(p.44)* • **Upright:** Masculinity, physical strength, determination, capability, skill. **Reversed:** Impotence, physical weakness, hesitation, inability.

3. THURISAZ *(p.46)* • **Upright:** Protection, obstacle, defense, caution, patience. **Reversed:** Recklessness, impatience, bad news, false promises.

1. FEHU *(p.42)* • **Upright:** Wealth, status, property, financial gain, vitality. **Reversed:** Poverty, loss of esteem or wealth, apathy.

4. ANSUZ *(p.48)* • **Upright:** Good advice, learning, authority, communication. **Reversed:** Bad advice, misjudgment, deceit or trickery from someone in authority.

5. RAIDO *(p.50)* • **Upright:** Travel, progress, change. **Reversed:** Immobility, delay, difficult journey, regression.

6. KENAZ *(p.52)* • **Upright:** Warmth, celebration, love, success, light, creativity. **Reversed:** Failure, loss, end of passion, darkness, lack of inspiration.

7. GEBO *(p.54)* • **Upright:** Giving, receiving, love match, partnership, opportunity. **No reversal.**

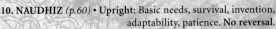

8. WUNJO *(p.56)* • **Upright:** Joy, celebration, luck, harmony, family. **Reversed:** Sadness, bad luck, conflict, hindrances, loss of affection.

9. HAGALAZ *(p.58)* • **Upright:** Shock, damage, unpredictability, arbitrary disruption. **No reversal.**

10. NAUDHIZ *(p.60)* • **Upright:** Basic needs, survival, invention, adaptability, patience. **No reversal.**

11. ISA *(p.62)* • **Upright:** Standstill, thwarted plans, leisure break, recharging of batteries. **No reversal.**

12. JERA *(p.64)* • **Upright:** Harvest, reward, renewal, birth, new beginning. **No reversal.**

Reversed runes are runes that are upside down. They usually have the opposite, or reverse, of their standard meaning. Some runes do not have reversals because they are identical upright and reversed.

23. OTHILA *(p.86)* • **Upright:** Inheritance, home, homeland, family property. **Reversed:** Property and financial disputes.

22. INGWAZ *(p.84)* • **Upright:** Potency, latent energy, orgasm, fruition, goal. **No reversal.**

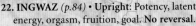

21. LAGUZ *(p.82)* • **Upright:** Intuition, imagination, creativity, fluidity. **Reversed:** Confusion, lack of imagination, stagnation.

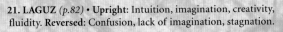

20. MANNAZ *(p.80)* • **Upright:** The self, individual family member, relationship, intelligence. **Reversed:** Isolation, greed, selfishness, egocentricity.

24. DAGAZ *(p.88)* • **Upright:** Clarity, openness, increase, positive start. **No reversal.**

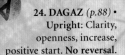

19. EHWAZ *(p.78)* • **Upright:** Transport, career change, control, partnership. **Reversed:** Travel problems, lack of control, cancellation.

18. BERKANA *(p.76)* • **Upright:** Nurturing, growth, fertility, beauty, healing. **Reversed :** Self-delusion, stagnation, emotional upheaval, infertility.

17. TEIWAZ *(p.74)* • **Upright:** Victory, honor, justice, balance. **Reversed:** Struggle, frustration, legal or emotional problems.

16. SOWILU *(p.72)* • **Upright:** Success, wholeness, vitality, good fortune, popularity. **No reversal.**

15. ALGIZ *(p.70)* • **Upright:** Protection, sanctuary, prayer, friendship, trust, faith. **Reversed:** Danger, stress, vulnerability, deception.

14. PERTHO *(p.68)* • **Upright:** Mystery, karma, chance, unpredictable event, exposure. **Reversed:** Chaos, harmful secret, disempowerment, disappointment.

13. EIHWAZ *(p.66)* • **Upright:** Flexibility, endurance, protection, empowerment, resolution. **No reversal.**

Many runecasters prefer to ignore reversals, believing that there are sufficient positive and negative meanings in the standard rune interpretations to give a full and detailed reading. Some runemasters only use reversals for certain types of runecast. You could even select a single rune before each runecast to decide. If it is reversed, then incorporate reversed runes into your reading; if not, don't. Experience will guide you toward the methods that best suit your purposes. The above summary of upright and reversed meanings (note that the runes are shown in their reversed positions) will help you to interpret the runes you cast, although you should refer to Chapter Two for greater insight (see pages 40–89).

runecasts

The term casting refers to an ancient method of divination whereby bundles of sticks, bones, or similar objects were thrown onto the ground and then interpreted in relation to the way in which they fell.

Instead of throwing the runes in this way, many modern runemasters prefer to select a specific number of runes at random and place them into set positions known as runecasts. The number of runes you use and the positions in which you place them will depend on the particular runecast you are using. Four examples are given here. Once you become familiar with the dynamics of runecasting, you can invent different runecasts of your own, allowing you to customize readings to suit any purpose.

1 ONE-RUNE DRAW
The one-rune draw gives a quick overview or response to a current situation.

EXAMPLE I

"Can I trust this new friend of mine?"
If Algiz were drawn, the answer would be unequivocally affirmative because Algiz represents protection, trust, and friendship. Should Hagalaz be drawn, however, the querent should be cautious because this rune's primary meanings are destruction and disaster.

2 THE NORNIC ORACLE

This simple runecast involves selecting three runes to represent the Nornir (see pages 38–39). The first is the Urd rune, symbolizing the past; the second is the Verdandi rune, representing the present; and the third is the Skuld rune, signifying the future. The Nornic oracle can be applied to any situation to provide an indication of the influences that have brought the situation about, the influences that currently predominate, and the likely outcome of the matter.

(see pages 38–39)

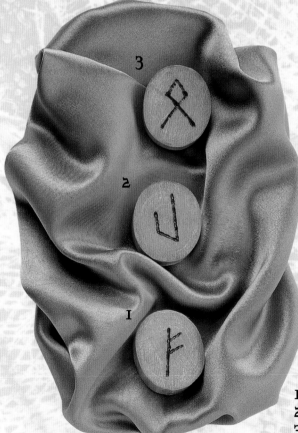

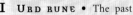

1 **URD RUNE** • The past
2 **VERDANDI RUNE** • The present
3 **SKULD RUNE** • The future

3 THOR'S CROSS

This runecast uses five runes laid out in the form of a simple cross. The four arms of the cross represent the four cardinal directions and the four elements, while the center symbolizes the quintessence or spirit. In Nordic tradition, the four directions are named after the four dwarfs that support the vault of heaven (the giant Ymir's skull). The dwarfs are Sudri (south), Westri (west), Nordri (north), and Austri (east). When using this runecast, place the first rune in the south position to represent the general influences affecting the situation. Working clockwise, place the second rune in the west, indicating the obstacles faced. The third rune, in the north, signifies favorable influences. The fourth rune, in the east, indicates the likely outcome. Place the fifth rune in the center. This denotes the presiding influence over the whole situation and gives an indication of the long-term significance of the situation or the nature of the lesson to be learned.

EXAMPLE 3

"Should I take this opportunity to live in another country?"
The south rune selected is Raido, which, appropriately, indicates change or a journey and suggests progress. The west rune is Pertho, the mystery rune, suggesting that there are no obvious obstacles and that any difficulties arising will be because the querent has failed to generate sufficient good will with the universe. The north rune is Thurisaz, which, in this position, is very favorable, indicating that Thor himself is on the querent's side. The east rune is Isa, the ice rune that freezes all plans and thwarts all progress, forcing the querent to remain stationary. With an indication as unequivocal as this, the querent has no choice but to abandon any plans of moving for the foreseeable future, particularly with the immovable object of Thurisaz blocking any wrong move. The central rune is Fehu, suggesting that the greatest opportunities for success, creativity, wealth, and security lie where the querent currently resides.

BELOW A Viking headdress in the shape of Mjollnir, the thunder-striking hammer that was forged by dwarfs for the god Thor.

I SUDRI RUNE • General influences
2 WESTRI RUNE • Obstacles faced
3 NORDRI RUNE • Favorable influences
4 AUSTRI RUNE • Likely outcome
5 SPIRIT RUNE • Long-term significance

3

NORDRI
(NORTH)

2

WESTRI
(WEST)

5

SPIRIT

4

AUSTRI
(EAST)

1

SUDRI
(SOUTH)

5 **THE CROWN**

The best that can be achieved or attained from current circumstances.

THE CROSS

Current obstacles, problems, conflicts, and opposition that the querent must deal with.

10 **THE OUTCOME**

The long-term outcome of the situation or the lesson that can be learned from it.

4 **THE PAST**

Events or influences from the recent past that are now passing away.

2

9 **THE HOPES AND FEARS**

The querent's hopes, fears, and expectations with regard to the question or the current situation.

1

THE PRESENT

The predominating events, issues, attitudes, or influences around the question or current situation.

6 **THE FUTURE**

Future events and fresh influences about to come into play.

8 **THE HOUSE**

How people around the querent affect and view matters in hand.

3 **THE ROOT**

The basis or root cause of the current situation.

7 **THE QUERENT**

How the querent relates to the situation in question.

4 THE CELTIC CROSS

This spread is widely used for tarot readings and works very well with the runes, providing a good balance of the dynamics that come to play in almost any situation. It consists of ten runes.

EXAMPLE 4

"Should I start my own business?"

1. The Present: Pertho suggests that this is a moment when the universe is going to allow the querent to reap what he or she has sown. Whether this harvest will be sweet or bitter remains to be seen.

2. The Cross: Ehwaz reversed indicates that there is a tricky obstacle to overcome. Ehwaz relates to partnerships, so there may be a problem with a partner or associate.

3. The Root: Sowilo reveals that the proposed business venture is inspired by the querent's good fortune, popularity, or sheer vitality.

4. The Past: Eihwaz signifies that the querent may have recently been empowered by his or her flexibility, resolve, or prowess at problem solving.

5. The Crown: Uruz is ideal for high-risk ventures and suggests that the querent should seize this opportunity with determination.

6. The Future: Thurisaz indicates that, if the querent proceeds with patience and caution, he or she should have no insurmountable problem.

7. The Querent: Dagaz shows that the querent has a clear grasp of the business, that there are no hidden obstacles, and that the financial prospects are bright.

8. The House: Fehu indicates that the people around the querent are very positive and have good business sense.

9. The Hopes and Fears: Wunjo reversed implies that the querent greatly fears that a business partner may let him or her down. The previous rune, however, reveals that this fear is unfounded.

10. The Outcome: Mannaz reversed seems confusing at first. This would normally indicate that the querent is surrounded by negatively motivated people, but since the House rune showed the reverse, the inference to be drawn is that the querent is being unnecessarily suspicious and that the problem is imagined. Referring back to the Cross rune, it is clear that the querent must overcome any misgivings about a prospective partner. If he or she does so, the prospects are good; if not, there will be no progress.

RUNE
MAGIC

THE ANCIENT GERMANIC PEOPLES HAD A
MAGICAL WORLDVIEW. THE GREAT NORSE SAGAS
ARE FULL OF FASCINATING SNIPPETS OF MAGIC,
MUCH OF WHICH INVOLVES USING THE RUNES
AS POWERFUL TALISMANS. OTHER MAGICAL
USES FOR THE RUNES INCLUDE INCANTATIONS
AND WRITTEN PETITIONS.

meditation

most magicians and runemasters believe that the universe is a conscious entity with which we can communicate through the use of symbols such as runes.

Meditation is one way of initiating this communication. You will need to practice for at least 10–15 minutes each day to become proficient. Assume a comfortable sitting position, close your eyes, and spend a few minutes concentrating on your breathing. Keeping it slow and steady, begin to deepen your breath and consciously relax your body. When you are relaxed, pick a runestone at random and concentrate on it. When you are sufficiently receptive, the runes can send you messages that help you progress along the path to self-discovery.

THE WAY OF THE WYRD

Wyrd is a Norse concept for destiny. Wyrd shares the same linguistic root as the modern German *wird*, meaning will be; *wert*, meaning value; and *wurde*, meaning worth. It is also connected with the English word weird, which means uncanny or strange. The Weird Sisters in Shakespeare's *Macbeth* come from the Norse tradition of the Nornir. They are symbols of fate rather than evil. They are not responsible for the crimes that Macbeth commits, but they foresee them and allow them to unfold, for they spin the web of life with the yarn of human actions. Wyrd, therefore, is not an inescapable, arbitrary fate, but one that we affect by our actions.

SELF-DISCOVERY

The way of the Wyrd is a path that will lead to self-discovery and every human being has the opportunity to walk along that path. Herein lies the significance of the other root meanings of Wyrd—value and worth. If you can perceive the true value of things and be worthy in your deeds, you will come closer to understanding your life purpose. By randomly selecting a rune, you are allowing the Wyrd to send you a message and lead you on your spiritual path. That is when the wonder of the Wyrd can be perceived—that eerie sense that you are mysteriously connected to all things.

LEFT & OPPOSITE Shakespeare's Weird Sisters symbolize the Nornir and fate. By meditating on the runes, you can receive messages to help you reach your true destiny—self-discovery.

Runic blessings

Runic blessings use magical incantations to summon the qualities of a particular rune. By evoking a rune such as wunjo, for example, you can attract joy and harmony to your own or someone else's life.

This form of magic is known as *galdr*, which means incantation. It is often combined with *stadha*, the use of ritual body positions for magical purposes. Both of these practices are used in many different magical traditions around the world.

INVOKING ODIN

Before evoking the runes through chanting, it is wise to align yourself with the power that made them available—the great runemaster Odin. You can honor him and invoke Odinic energy by assuming the Algiz rune position, with your eyes and arms raised to the heavens, and incanting:

O
Odin,
All-father,
All-seeing, all-wise,
Whose knowledge is gleaned
From the Earth, seas, and skies,
Help me evoke the power of this rune,
May it act as a lodestone and bring me a boon.

LEFT When invoking the power of Odin, stand in the Algiz rune position with your eyes and arms raised.

ETHICS

Rune magic should be used wisely and efficiently. It is best to work within your capacity and allow your magical abilities to grow over time. Also consider the nature of your intent when working rune magic. The runes activate powerful forces. When misused, they can cause harm.

EVOKING THE RUNES

You can evoke the power of a rune by incanting words and sounds associated with its phonetic correspondence. To send a blessing of Wunjo energy to a friend, for example, imagine the person smiling in the sunshine, in a glade surrounded by ash trees, amid joyful well-wishers carrying golden flags shaped like Wunjo. A good incantation would be:

ABOVE Carry golden flags shaped like the Wunjo rune and chant alliterative rhymes to send a blessing of Wunjo joy to a loved one. The ash is connected with Wunjo, so perform the blessing in a glade of ash trees if possible.

We, we, we wish you wonderful, wunjoful joy.
We, we, we wish you well, wonderful, wunjoful joy.

If the person is with you, take him or her by the hand while performing the chant and dance around in a celebratory circle. The more you repeat this ritual, the greater the amount of Wunjo power you can send someone's way.

Runic Talismans

A runic talisman is a ritually prepared object that uses runic symbols to achieve specific results. Runestones are powerful talismans in themselves, but there are ways in which you can customize them to suit specific purposes.

The simplest form of runic talisman is a runestone. You can evoke its power using incantations (see pages 114–115) and then simply keep it nearby, either in a pocket, bag, or on a cord around your neck. For example, you could wear the Algiz rune for personal protection or Fehu to attract wealth. More complex talismans can be made using two or more runes together. You can use many different materials to make a talisman, such as metal, clay, wax, cardboard, or paper.

HOUSE PROTECTION TALISMAN

If you wish to protect your house while you are away on vacation, Thurisaz (protection) and Othila (home) would be suitable runes. Inscribe the Othila rune in the middle of a piece of white cardboard. This can be done in black or in the color that corresponds with Othila, which is yellow. Then inscribe the Thurisaz rune in either black or red (the color that corresponds with Thurisaz) above, below, and to the left and right of Othila. The talisman represents your home surrounded by a forest of thorns, like that around Sleeping Beauty's castle. Pin the talisman to a bulletin board near the heart of the home, such as the kitchen, ideally using the thorns of a blackthorn or hawthorn tree, which correspond to Thurisaz and Othila respectively. Take care that the talisman is the right way up. If this ritual is performed with consciously focused intent, it will give your home effective protection. However, beware the little tricks of the Wyrd. On returning home you may find that all is safe and sound, but you have lost your keys and are barred from access.

OPPOSITE Protect your home while you are away on vacation by leaving a talisman featuring Othila and Thurisaz runes pinned to a bulletin board.

BINDRUNES

Bindrunes are two or more runes joined together to form a powerful magical sigil. These sigils, or signs, are ideally suited to talismanic magic. A selection of bindrunes is pictured below, but you can combine any runes you wish in any design you find pleasing. Runes are usually easy to join together because they are angular in design. One popular bindrune design is based on a simple cross shape, with a rune at the end of each point on the cross and sometimes a rune at the center point. When designing this type of bindrune, you might like to think about the four elements with which each rune is associated and place them in the appropriate location on the cross—north is connected with earth, east with air, south with fire, and west with water. The center of the cross represents the spirit or essence, so this is a good place to put the rune that is most significant for the talisman. Another popular design for bindrunes is an eight-spoked wheel. Runes can be written along and at the end of each spoke as well as at the center of the wheel. Some runemasters also write a runic message around the circumference of the wheel.

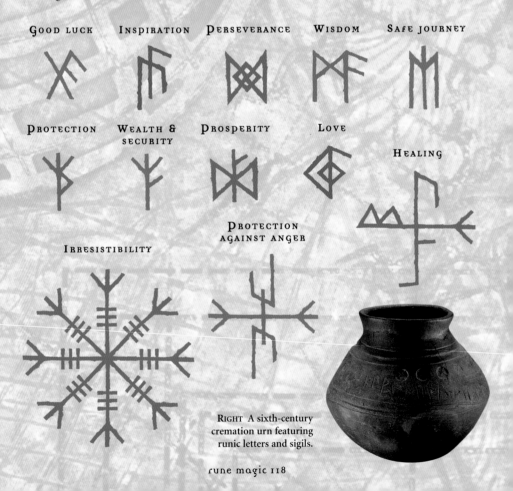

GOOD LUCK   INSPIRATION   PERSEVERANCE   WISDOM   SAFE JOURNEY

PROTECTION   WEALTH & SECURITY   PROSPERITY   LOVE

HEALING

IRRESISTIBILITY

PROTECTION AGAINST ANGER

RIGHT A sixth-century cremation urn featuring runic letters and sigils.

MAGICAL TOOLS

Individual runes and bindrunes can be inscribed into magical tools and objects such as wands, knives, and rings in order to empower them. In ancient times, such inscriptions could often be found on weapons. For example, shields were inscribed with runes of protection so that, in effect, the shield became a talisman that would protect its bearer during battle. Swords would be given a suitably warlike name and this would be inscribed in runic lettering onto the sword's hilt or blade in order to empower the weapon with the runes' qualities. When using a knife to carve a set of runestones, you may wish to give the knife a runic name and inscribe this onto its hilt. Wands are used to direct magical energy, so by inscribing specific runes along the length of a wand, you can empower it with their associated qualities. Meditation is a good way of choosing suitable runes for this purpose (see pages 112–113).

ABOVE & LEFT Runic inscriptions are frequently found on tools, weaponry, and armor, such as this Anglo-Saxon helmet from Sutton Hoo, England. You may wish to inscribe suitable runic designs onto your own magical tools.

runic
wishes

BY writing your wish on a piece of paper, you can encourage it to come true. The act of writing involves more concentrated effort than simply speaking a wish, and therefore carries more of your energy.

ABOVE To make a runic wish for love, draw the Gebo rune on a piece of blue cardboard, concentrating on your desire as you do so.

Wishes can be written on a plain piece of white paper or you can use a color that corresponds with your wish. For example, if you want to attract a lover, you could use blue paper because that color corresponds with the Gebo rune, which is associated with love and partnerships. Focus your attention on your desired goal and write down the runic symbols that best represent your wish. Alternately, translate your wish letter by letter into runic script. Although ancient runic writing ran from right to left, there is no need to do this unless you want to. Sit quietly for a few minutes, concentrating on what you have written. Keep the paper in a safe place, reading it occasionally if you want to. If your wish is fulfilled or no longer applies, you can burn it with gratitude, thereby dissolving its energy.

TRANSLATING ENGLISH INTO RUNES

Petitioning the gods

Wishes written in runic script have more resonance and are more clearly understood by the Norse gods. To petition a Norse god to grant a wish, first establish which god is responsible for the matter at hand (see Chapter One, pages 16–39). For example, to attract a lover, you could petition Baldur, the Norse god of love, light, and beauty. Simply write: "In the name of the most beloved Baldur, I ask that …" Write the petition in runic script but sign it with your usual signature. Put your petition in an envelope together with any relevant items, such as a photograph, a flower petal, or a pinch of incense—whatever you feel may help the gods tune in to your request. Writing a petition requires a calm, quiet mind and dedicated concentration.

BELOW Translate your wish into runic script to petition the Norse gods for their help in making it come true.

annual festivals

norse magic is essentially natural magic. it is based on a deep rapport with natural forces and rhythms, so to perform norse magic most effectively, you need to affirm your relationship with nature.

The Germanic peoples celebrated their relationship with nature communally at the eight great solar and fire festivals. The eternal rhythm of nature is played out in an annual cycle as one year flows into another. This cycle was seen by the Germanic peoples as the annual sacrifice and resurrection of the Sun, without which there would be no seasons. The eight festivals punctuated this annual cycle like spokes on the solar wheel. By marking these eight festivals with appropriate rituals, you can bring yourself into harmonious rhythm with nature. Traditionally, the Sun is honored as it sets, then a ritual fire is lit and tended through the night, around which people dance, sing, tell stories, and make merry with feasting and games. The end of the vigil is marked by the return of the Sun, which is honored as the life-giving light of the world.

LEFT The ancient Germanic tribes celebrated the solar cycle at eight annual festivals. This Bronze Age Chariot of the Sun was discovered in Denmark in 1902 and features a horse pulling a gilded Sun disk on a chariot.

WINTER SOLSTICE

The winter solstice occurs around December 21st/22nd and is the time of the shortest day and the longest darkness in the Northern Hemisphere. For the Germanic tribes, the year began at the winter solstice, symbolizing the death and rebirth of the Sun. It was celebrated as a great fire festival known as Yule, from the Norse word *Jol*, when enormous Yule logs were burned for 12 days to feed the fire of the Sun. Many of the old Yule customs were incorporated into Christmas tradition—the Christmas tree, for example, is a representation of Yggdrasil. This is a good time to write runic wishes for the year ahead.

IMBOLC

The next festival is celebrated around February 1st/2nd and marks the beginning of spring. It is dedicated to the hearth, the heart of the home. Traditionally, the hearth is ritually toasted by its beneficiaries and a small libation of ale is thrown on it. This is the time for sowing and planting to begin, so you could make a Fehu talisman and bury it in a plant pot or your garden to attract prosperity to your home.

SPRING EQUINOX

The next festival is spring equinox on March 20th/21st, when day begins to outlast night. This was usually celebrated by the Germanic tribes to honor Ostara/Oestre, the spring goddess of the dawn whose symbols, the hare and the cosmic egg, became the Easter bunny and Easter egg. It marks the peak of spring energies and renewed growth, when day and night are equal and in balance. It is a good time to evoke or meditate on the Dagaz rune, which represents a new cycle of growth.

index

credits

Quarto would like to thank and acknowledge the following for images reproduced in this book:

Key: t = top, b = bottom, l = left, r = right, c = center,

6bl Topham Picturepoint, 7b Heritage-Images/British Museum, 9 Art Directors and Trip/Eric Smith, 13tr Topham Picturepoint, 15tr Topham/Fotomas, 18br Ann Ronan Picture Library, 27 Ann Ronan Picture Library, 28tl Topham Picturepoint, 31 Topham Picturepoint, 35t Topham Picturepoint, 37tc Ann Ronan Picture Library, 38br Ann Ronan Picture Library, 39t Ann Ronan Picture Library, 45cl Topham/Fotomas, 48br Art Directors and Trip/Jean King, 49c Topham Picturepoint, 51t Art Directors and Trip/Eric Smith, 53t Heritage-Images/British Museum, 60 Ann Ronan Picture Library, 61cl Topham/Fotomas, 67 Art Directors and Trip/H. Rogers, 70 Art Directors and Trip/J. Braund, 72b Martin J. Powell (http://homepage.ntlworld.com/mjpowell/index.htm), 76–77b Art Directors and Trip/F. Blackburn, 77tl Topham/Keystone, 79tr Charles & Josette Lenars/Corbis, 83br Topham/ Fotomas, 85t Art Directors and Trip/H. Rogers, 86–87b Art Directors and Trip/N. Price, 94cl Art Directors and Trip/H. Rogers, 95tl Art Directors and Trip/H. Rogers, 95br Art Directors and Trip/H. Rogers, 118br Heritage-Images/British Museum, 119cl Ann Ronan Picture Library, 123t Ann Ronan Picture Library, 124tl Art Directors and Trip/H. Rogers, 125br Art Directors and Trip/H. Rogers.

All other photographs and illustrations are the copyright of Quarto. While every effort has been made to credit contributors, we apologize should there be any omissions or errors.